HOPE
is
ETERNAL

100 DEVOTIONS FOR WOMEN. GOD'S GOT THIS

Eileen Nyberg

TABLE OF CONTENTS

INTRODUCTION

Everyone goes through hard times in their lives. Everyone struggles at one time or another. There will be days when you feel as though you can't take another step. But there is good news. A relationship with God can help change your life for the best. When you know Him, you can trust Him and turn to Him at any time. No matter the hard times, you can always find rest, relief, and reassurance in His presence. Jesus is the hope that you can cling to no matter how bleak things seem. He can and will work something out for your good and the glory of His Kingdom. He wants to be your hope and to reassure you that things will turn out alright. He wants you to find rest in His presence in the good times and amazing times, not just when things are too difficult to handle.

His hope can turn your darkest day around and change your thought pattern from, "why is this happening to me?" to, "I know God's got this. I know He will get me through whatever situation that comes my way."

You can have hope in the things you do not see and the hope that He will provide for you in every area of your life. The hard times will not last. Things will get better in your life. You are never alone. You are never far away from Him and His love. He invites you to call on His name at any time, anywhere. There is always something to hope for. Keep His promises close to your heart. He wants to give you hope for your future. Cling to the one, true, everlasting hope that you can only find in Jesus.

HOW TO USE THIS BOOK

You can use this easy-to-read 100-day devotional of hope and prayer to help you have hope in the midst of your dark times. You will find short scriptures of hope that will fill you with the reassurance that you need to keep going when times get rough—having hope can change your outlook about life in many different ways. This book is designed to give you the everlasting hope of God's promises when you need them the most.

Each devotional contains a daily scripture of hope, then an easy-to-understand explanation of each scripture. Finally, there is a powerful prayer of relief that you can pray after reading each devotional to help you release His hope into your heart. Each devotional and prayer offers you the opportunity to spend more one-on-one time with God and get to know Him on a deeper level.

We hope that this devotional will help you cling to the hope you can find in Jesus, no matter what you may be going through.

Nothing Can Separate You from God

"Who shall separate us from the love of Christ? Shall trouble or hardship or persecution or famine or nakedness or danger or sword?"
Romans 8:35 NIV

No matter what may be going on in your life, nothing can separate you from the love of Christ. Whatever hardships you are going through, you can rely on Christ to get you through them. He is with you at all times. You can find comfort in the fact that God knows all of the tribulations you will face before you even face them. He also has a solution to every one of your problems before they even begin. Even though the problems you face may seem huge to you, they are so tiny compared to God's ability to do great things in your life. Your problems are minuscule compared to God's love for you! Whenever things seem to be too hard to handle, and you face hardships such as persecution for being a Christian, hunger, or facing any sort of danger, you can rest in the assurance that God will protect you and be with you.

You may have thought that you aren't lovable because of your sin. No matter how you have sinned, God still loves you as His child. He wants you to know how special you are to Him. Nothing you have done or will do will ever stop His love for you.

Prayer for Worried:
Dear God, thank you that nothing can ever separate me from
your love. Thank you that you're with me at every stage of my life.
Please help me to focus on you when the daily stress threatens
to overwhelm me. Thank you for loving me even though I'm a
sinner. Please remind me to trust you no matter what's happening.

Firm Place to Stand

*"I waited patiently for the Lord; he turned to me and heard my
cry. He lifted me out of the slimy pit, out of the mud and mire;
he set my feet on a rock and gave me a firm place to stand."*
Psalm 40:1

Waiting patiently isn't easy for anyone. You can learn to wait patiently for God when things don't seem to be going the way you'd like. Waiting patiently for God takes practice at every stage of life. You want life to go well, but sometimes, things just fall apart. It can be discouraging when it feels like God isn't listening to your prayers.

But you can trust that God hears all of your prayers, no matter how big or small they are. Pray boldly over everything in your life. Then wait patiently for Him to answer. God will give you guidance in every area of your life. He hears you when you cry out to Him in the middle of your darkest hour of despair. He is never deaf to your prayers. He never ignores your feelings. Even when you can't feel or see Him working on things, He always works behind the scenes. He will lift you out of your darkest times and give you a firm place to stand in His love. He is the solid rock that you can build your life around. Trust that He hears the deepest cries of your heart. No matter how hopeless things seem, He is working on your behalf.

Prayer of Gratitude:
Dear Lord, thank you that you've lifted me out of my
dark times and that you will do it again. Thank you
for always listening to me and for hearing my prayers.
Thank you for giving me a firm place to stand.

WEAK TO STRONG

"But God chose the foolish things of the world to shame the wise;
God chose the weak things of the world to shame the strong."
1 Corinthians 1:27

God empowers you. He can use the insecurities you have and the doubts you experience in your life in some of the most amazing ways. You might see your insecurities as faults, but God never looks at your faults. God sees you as His beloved child. Even though you will feel weak at times, God can use your weaknesses to make you stronger. Through hard times, you can learn some of the most valuable lessons. Even when you feel weak, God is working within you. You are His handiwork.

God can use you in mighty ways. Even when you feel uncertain, He can help you make wise decisions. He can make you stronger through any trial that you face. Even when you feel as though you may not be able to make an impact for His kingdom, all you have to do is be yourself and share the hope that you have in your heart. You can tell others about the hope of God and how that hope has changed your life. God empowers and equips you to speak about the hope that you have at just the right time. God chose you to be a witness for His kingdom. He empowers you to tell everyone how He has impacted your life. Embrace the opportunity to point others to Christ.

PRAYER FOR HELP:
Dear Lord, thank you for empowering me to speak about the
hope that you have given me in my life. Help me to not feel
weak or discouraged when telling others about You. Help
me to share how you've changed my life with gladness.

DELIVERED FROM TROUBLE

"The righteous cry out, and the Lord hears them; he delivers them from all their troubles... The righteous person may have many troubles, but the Lord delivers him from them all."
Psalm 34:17

No matter how big or small your prayers, God hears them all. If you cry out to Him in the stillness of your heart, He hears you. If you cry out to God out loud, He hears you. Even though you will have troubles in your life, God can and will deliver you from them all. All you have to do is cry out and ask Him for His help. He will gladly give you the desires of your heart as long as they are in line with His will. When you cry out to Him, you can cling to the hope and the promise that He hears everything that's on your mind. He sees your tears and knows your fears before you even speak them.

No matter the troubles you face, you can have the hope and confidence that God will deliver you from each one of them. He may let you go through some difficult times, but He does that to strengthen your reliance on Him. God hears your cries, no matter where you are, how old you are, and even if you don't speak a word of your struggles out loud. God knows what you are going through and what you will go through. He has a wonderful plan to deliver you from your troubles. He always cares about you.

PRAYER OF COMFORT:
Dear God, thank you for delivering me from all my troubles.
Thank you for hearing my prayers, whether they are spoken or not.
Thank you for listening to me and for always caring about me.

Pour Out Your Heart to God

*"Trust in him at all times, you people; pour out
your hearts to him, for God is our refuge."*
Psalm 62:8 NIV

God is your refuge and ever-present help in times of trouble. You can trust in Him at all times and hope in His plan for your life. Even with COVID-19 being rampant in our world, God has still delivered us and allowed us to get a vaccine that helps protect against the spread of the virus. Because of God's mercy, you can now get together with friends and family again. Learning to trust God hasn't been easy in these testing times, but it has helped people rely on Him for everything.

You don't have to be afraid of pouring out your heart to Him whenever you feel you can't go on. You may have lost hope in the midst of Covid-19 being rampant in our world since 2020. You have probably missed your family and spending time with your friends. But isolation also allowed you to get closer to God. Did you take that opportunity to read His word and spend time with Him every day? Did you cling to the promise that God would protect you and your family from the virus? Whenever you feel the weight of this world is too much for you to handle, come to Him. Cry out to Him for hope, reassurance, and peace. Ask for His hope to fill your heart and watch how He intervenes.

PRAYER FOR GUIDANCE:
Dear God, thank you for slowing the spread of Covid-19.
Thank you for allowing me to be with my friends and family again.
Please continue to protect us from the virus. Help me to remember
to always trust in you even when things in life look bleak.

An Anchor for the Soul

"We have this hope as an anchor for the soul, firm and secure….
Where our forerunner, Jesus, has entered on our behalf…."
Hebrews 6:19-20 NIV

Hope is the true anchor for the soul, especially when times get tough. Jesus is the hope you can cling to when things get to be too much to handle. Jesus is the most important person in your life. He can lift you when you are feeling down. He can put a smile on your face when you feel like crying. He is the one who whispers with His Holy Spirit, "try again, my child," when you feel as if you are at your breaking point. He is also the one who comforts you with His loving and everlasting arms when you are breaking down from stress. He is there to pick you up when you feel as though you can't stand on your own two feet.

Hope is the anchor of all living things. It is what you can cling to when you are not sure what to think or if you're uncertain of what step to take next. Hoping in Jesus can make you feel warm, safe, and secure. When you enter His presence, your mood can instantly be lifted, and you can feel refreshed. He is preparing a glorious place for you in eternity with Him. Jesus has secured a place in heaven on your behalf. No matter what you're facing, you can cling to His hope as the anchor for your soul each day.

Prayer of Comfort:
Dear Lord, thank you for being my hope and my anchor, no matter what I'm facing. Please help me to remember that you have a place waiting for me in heaven. Thank you for being my safe place.

NO SHAME

"And hope does not put us to shame, because God's
love has been poured out into our hearts through
the Holy Spirit, who has been given to us."
Romans 5:5 NIV

Hope is the emotion that carries you through your whole life, especially when times are difficult. You may have been made fun of for trying to keep hope in your heart. People may have asked you why you decide to keep hoping for a better tomorrow, despite the hard times you're going through.

You can explain to them that your true hope is found in Jesus. You can also share this Bible verse. Jesus doesn't put you to shame for having hope in your heart. Hope won't ever put you to shame either. Hope doesn't put anyone to shame because hope is designed and orchestrated by God to have positive impacts on people's lives.

God loves everyone so much that He sent His one and only Son, Jesus, to die for us on the cross as a symbol of the hope to come when we reach heaven. God loves us so much that He poured out His love into our hearts by blessing us with the gift of the Holy Spirit dwelling within us. So, the next time you go through a rough patch in life, remember that you have a right-hand person that you can turn to for guidance, wisdom, hope, and strength-Jesus. You don't ever have to be ashamed to be hopeful in any circumstance.

PRAYER FOR GUIDANCE:
Dear Lord, please help me not be ashamed of having
hopeful thoughts or acting hopeful in any area of my life.
Thank you that it's OK to be hopeful in life. Help me to
remember that you're my number one source of hope.

Faith to Hope for Tomorrow

*"Now faith is confidence in what we hope for
and assurance about what we do not see."*
Hebrews 11:1 NIV

Having faith and keeping the faith during difficult times is a hard thing to remember. You may be confused as to how to keep the faith in the middle of uncertain times. Faith is confidence in everything you hope for. You can always hope for a better tomorrow despite the rough times that you might be facing. But you have to make a conscious effort in telling yourself, "Despite the way things look, everything will work out. Despite how exhausted I feel, I know God has a beautiful plan for my life." You have to train your mind to rise above your circumstances. Try your best not to let your circumstances dictate how you feel every day. It isn't something that you just learn overnight.

Faith can give you the hope that you need in life. Ask God to help you stay focused on Him. Look at the many blessings of life instead of dwelling on the things that stress you out. Faith is the everlasting and blessed assurance about the things that you don't see. That means that even though you don't physically see God, you can feel His presence at any time. You can see His beauty in the world around you in the face of a child laughing and in the beauty of a sunset. Even though you can't see Him, you can trust that He is working in your life.

Prayer for Help:
Dear God, please help me to stay focused on you
instead of stressing about my life. Please help me to
see the works of your hand in everything around me.
Help me to rest assured in your everlasting hope.

GOD OF HOPE

"May the God of hope fill you with all joy and peace
as you trust in him, so that you may overflow
with hope by the power of the Holy Spirit."
Romans 15:13 NIV

God is the God of everlasting hope. He can fill you with all the joy and peace that your heart has been longing for. He is willing and waiting to give you hope. Talk to Him, saying, "Lord, please help me to trust you despite what I'm feeling. Help me to focus on you instead of dwelling on the things I can't control. Please change my view of life from doom to a view of peace, love, and understanding. Please help me to have your everlasting peace in my life."

God will fill you with joy that can't be expressed if you allow Him to work on your heart. It's a heavenly joy that can only come from Him. You will feel lighter in your soul. Your mind will be more at ease as you work. You'll be able to focus on good things. The more you get to know Him, the more you will trust Him. You will feel His peace wash over you and embrace you like a warm blanket in the middle of tough trials. You will know that He has you in His hands and that He's guiding your every step. You will get to the point where you overflow with heavenly hope. It's the hope that will overflow within you by the power of the Holy Spirit.

PRAYER OF GRATITUDE:
Dear Lord, please help me to trust you instead of
focusing on things with my own power. Help me
to feel your peace as I rest assured in your plan for
my life. Thank you for your everlasting hope.

HOPE IN HIS NAME

"In his name the nations will put their hope."
Matthew 12:21 NIV

Having hope in God will change your life. You have to make a conscious effort to follow Him every day and try to honor Him in everything you do. If you put your hope in God, you will see His hand in everything you do in life. You will see His hand in your work, in your family life, and when you are with your friends. You will feel His presence when a friend or family member gives you a much-needed hug after a hard day at work. Instead of focusing on the bad things in your life, you will begin to see the beauty in your life. Even the littlest things will make you smile.

You will be able to seek Him in everything you do and make Him a priority in your life. He will bless you for following Him on a deeply personal level. He smiles on you whenever you pray, telling Him thank you for the blessings in your life. He also smiles on you whenever you bring your requests to Him, no matter how big or small they might be. He always wants to hear from you, no matter what you may be doing. You will sometimes forget to put your hope in Him, but He is always there for you. He is ready to guide you in the right direction, no matter how far you may have wandered from Him. Put your hope in Him and trust that no matter what happens, He is with you.

PRAYER FOR GUIDANCE:
Dear God, please help me to always remember to
put my hope in you. Help me turn back to you.
Thank you for guiding my every step.

Joyfully Hope

"Be joyful in hope, patient in affliction, faithful in prayer."
Romans 12:12 NIV

Being joyful in hope can be very difficult when you're in the midst of hard circumstances. You might be asking how you can possibly be joyful in hope when it feels as though there is nothing left to hope for. God wants you to be joyful despite the circumstances you find yourself in. There is always something to be thankful for, and there is always something to be happy about. All you have to do is look for the silver lining during your circumstances.

Being patient in affliction is another difficult task. You have probably asked yourself, "how does God expect me to be patient amid the affliction that I'm facing?" The good news is that God knows how hard it can be for you to remain patient. But He encourages you to find the strength to be patient by relying on Him.

Being faithful in prayer means thanking Him when things are going well. It also means coming before Him and boldly asking for things you need when life is tough. The best news is, God hears you when you're faithful in prayer. If you can learn to be faithful in prayer even when it feels like God doesn't hear you, you will experience His peace.

Prayer for Help:
Dear God, please help me be joyful despite hardships, keep hope in my heart, and be faithful in prayer no matter what is happening in my life. Thank you for always hearing my prayers. Please help me keep the hope in my heart that can only be found in you.

Hope in the Lord

"May integrity and uprightness protect me,
because my hope, Lord, is in you."
Psalm 25:21 NIV

Having integrity means being honest with yourself and those around you. It also means having strong morals. Having hope in the Lord is the most important thing to do in your life. If you have hope in anything, keep your hope in God Himself. After all, He is the only one who can and will bring you through any difficult times.

Having hope in the Lord means knowing that there is and will always be a way out of any scary or difficult circumstance that you face in your life. You can also pray that you stay the course of remaining close to God all the days of your life. Staying close to God throughout your life is so important. Being close to Him will help you in every aspect of your life. You can thank the Lord at any time and anywhere for giving you sound principles and morals. You can thank Him for guiding you in the right direction. You can also thank Him for being the hope that you can cling to no matter what you may be feeling. Whenever doubt starts to enter your mind about how you should handle a problem, turn to God and ask Him for the guidance you need. There is nothing wrong with admitting to God that you need His help. He will gladly help you. All you have to do is call on His name, and He will be there for you. He will help you stay honest with everyone around you.

PRAYER OF RELIEF:
Dear Lord, please help me to stay honest throughout
my life. Please help keep my morals sound. Thank you
that I can turn to you for anything and everything.

TAKE HEART

"Be strong and take heart, all you who hope in the Lord."
Psalm 31:24 NIV

You might be wondering how you can continually be strong and take heart in all that the Lord has done, will do, and is doing in your life, when you only see the problems looming in front of you. It can be difficult to focus on God when your problems seem to be too big to handle. There is much encouragement for you in this scripture, even in the middle of hard times. This scripture encourages you to be strong and take heart in the Lord because He is the one who can and will deliver you from any circumstances. God will not let you fall beyond His grip. He is always there for you whenever you need Him.

Even when you sometimes lose sight of Him, He is always there. Even when you lose sight of how He has helped you in the past and think that there is no possible way that He can or even will help you in your future, God wants you to remember that He has always been there for you. He will always be there for you. Ask Him to reveal His power in your life by reminding you of all the times He has been with you and delivered you from what you thought were impossible circumstances. If your hope is in Him, there is nothing He can't or won't do for you. Remember, it's hope that's gotten you this far in your life.

PRAYER FOR GUIDANCE:
Dear Lord, please help me to keep my hope in you.
Thank you for always being here for me. Thank you for
making a way when there seems to be no way.

Always Have Hope

"As for me, I will always have hope;
I will praise you more and more."
Psalm 71:14 NIV

You might be wondering how you can learn to praise God more no matter what you may be going through in your life. You can learn to have hope in your heart by reminding yourself that no matter how difficult things seem right now, everything will work out for you in life. You can remind yourself of how God has helped you overcome difficult things in your past and cling to the hope that He delivers you and will deliver you from anything that will happen to you in your future.

People will ask you why you seem so much happier and so much more at peace. Then you have the golden opportunity to tell them that your hope is found in Jesus. You can share your faith testimony and how God has helped you get through what you thought were impossible circumstances.

God allows you to share the reasons why you praise Him more and more every day. You can help others turn their lives around and start having the same hope you have in Jesus. Telling them the hope you have in the Lord can help them know that there is always something to be hopeful for. There is always something to hope in, and God is the source of all hope. So why not help someone else find the hope that they have longed for in their life for so long? Encourage others to turn to Jesus for hope.

Prayer for Guidance:
Dear Lord, please help me remember that I can always
have hope. Help me to lead others to you by professing
the hope that I have in and through you.

Be Bold in Hope

"Therefore, since we have such a hope, we are very bold."
2 Corinthians 3:12 NIV

People may have told you that there is no point in being bold in your life under any circumstances. On the contrary, God wants you to remember that having hope in Him gives you every opportunity to be bold.

You are allowed to proclaim His goodness in every area of your life, loudly and proudly. You are allowed to proclaim His goodness and mercy every day, no matter the circumstances you find yourself in. You can be bold in your prayers. He wants you to boldly pray for things. He wants you to have the confidence that you have already received the things you're praying for, even if it takes a while for those prayers to be answered. There is nothing wrong with praying for things as if you've already received them.

It might look and seem crazy to people who don't know God to pray boldly for things. They might even call you crazy. It just allows you to explain to them why you're so bold in prayer. Those who have a relationship with Him know exactly why you're acting and praying that way. You know that you should be bold enough to ask God for specifics in life. There is nothing wrong with believing that you will receive the things you ask for. Remember, if you ask for something in prayer and it aligns with His will, you will receive it.

Prayer for Guidance:
Dear God, please help me to want to boldly come before you in prayer. Help me believe that whatever I ask for in your name, I will receive it if it is your will. Thank you for the ability to hope boldly.

HOPE FROM GOD

"For God alone, O my soul, wait in silence, for my hope is from him."
Psalm 62:5 ESV

At times it can feel like you're waiting in silence for God to answer you. When you feel as though you are down to your last ounce of strength, that's when the thought of praying comes back to you. You shouldn't just turn God in prayer when it seems it's your last resort. You should want to pray all the time. God is the only reason you have made it this far in life. You may be waiting for God to do His handiwork in your life and waiting for Him to guide you about the next steps you have to take in your life. Even in the middle of waiting for Him, you can still come to Him in prayer and trust that He will never let you down.

You can have hope and faith in Him alone, trusting that His plan for your life is better than yours ever would be or could be. Even though it can seem as though you're waiting in silence, you can keep your hope in Him and trust that everything will work out according to His plan. Once you recognize that your unending hope comes from Him, you will be able to grab hold of that hope the next time Satan tries to knock you down. Instead of giving into him, remind him that God has already won the battle.

PRAYER OF GRATITUDE:
Dear God, please help me remember you and cling to the hope that you freely give me. Thank you that prayer can be one of the things that I do the most. Thank you for filling me with everlasting hope.

Living Hope

"Blessed be the God and Father of our Lord Jesus Christ! According to his great mercy, he has caused us to be born again to a living hope through the resurrection of Jesus Christ from the dead…"
1 Peter 1:3 ESV

No matter how difficult this life can be, you are God's beloved child. He set you apart and wants nothing but the best for you in your life. You were bought with His precious blood when He died for you on the cross at Calvary. You are now born again through faith in Jesus Christ. Jesus loves you enough that He willingly died for you on the cross, just to bring you salvation for all eternity. You now have the living hope of Jesus flowing through you every day of your life. Embrace the challenges that arise, knowing that God is with you and will help you through each obstacle. Nothing is too difficult for Him. Cling to the hope that you have through faith in Jesus Christ alone.

When you're tempted to feel discouraged or angry over the way things are going in your life, remember that you can be joyful instead. Remind yourself that you can be hopeful for the future that's ahead of you instead of dwelling on the mistakes you made in the past. Thank God for the opportunity to come before Him at any time, anywhere, no matter if you feel worthy to be in His presence or not. Thank God for the opportunity to learn something new every day, with Him leading you every step of the way.

Prayer for Comfort:
Dear Lord, thank you for dying on the cross to save my life. Thank you for filling me with your everlasting hope. Thank you that I'm your child.

HOPE THROUGH SCRIPTURE

"For whatever was written in former days was written for
our instruction, that through endurance and through the
encouragement of the Scriptures, we might have hope."
Romans 15:4 ESV

The Bible might seem like it is a waste of time to read. It can be so hard to understand, even with a group of friends or as an individual. When you read it, are you often left with more questions than answers? Who do you go to for help so you can understand His word better? This scripture points out that everything written in the Bible was written for your very own instruction. It was written as a guide as to how to live your life. It was also written as a way to help you get closer to God every time you read it.

The Bible isn't supposed to be a big book of rules that you need to follow. It's supposed to be the ultimate book. It's supposed to fill you with questions, inspire you beyond your wildest dreams, and fill you with the hope of God at the turn of every page. Sink into the most comfortable chair in your house, and let yourself be immersed in God's word. Let it enlighten, teach, and inspire you beyond what you ever thought possible. You can start small, reading a few verses. Ask God to help you learn more about Him daily through reading His word.

PRAYER FOR GUIDANCE:
Dear God, please help me to want to read your word more.
Thank you that I can read it any time I want. Allow me
to be immersed in it. Help me to feel your hope flowing
through me as I learn more about you every day.

HOPE OF GLORY

"To them God chose to make known how great among
the Gentiles are the riches of the glory of this mystery,
which is Christ in you, the hope of glory."
Colossians 1:27 ESV

You might be asking how you could have the hope of glory in you right now. With being a believer, you do have the glory of God and the riches of His glory within you at this very moment. God wants you to know the greatness of His love and mercy in this day and age, just as much as He did when the Bible was first starting to be written. He wants you and everyone to know how great He is, was, and will forever be.

The hope of glory is Christ in you. He is within your mind, body, soul, and spirit. God's glory is an unending mystery that will astound you every day of your life. All you have to do is look for Him, and you will see His beauty in everything, from the thunderous roar of a waterfall after a rainstorm to the beauty of the flowers in a field or the beauty of the leaves in the fall. You will feel the hope of His glory in you when you start recognizing your blessings in everyday life. Call them out by name and thank God for them, whether they are your family members, your job, car, or the ability to be away from work for the weekend. Embrace the hope that God gives you every day.

PRAYER FOR GUIDANCE:
Dear Lord, thank you for making your hope known to me. Thank
you that there's still so much for me to learn about you. Thank
you for revealing exactly what I need to know at the right time.

Confession of Hope

"Let us hold fast the confession of our hope without
wavering, for he who promised is faithful."
Hebrews 10:23 ESV

The confession of your hope can be a confusing thing to think about. When you confess with your mouth and heart that Jesus is the Lord over your life, it is something that takes hold of you while the excitement for God builds. However, that excitement for God gets drowned out so easily by the pressures of this world. You often forget that you should be confessing God's love to everyone when there are deadlines to meet at school or work or when there are financial concerns to worry about. Rather than holding fast to the confession of your hope without wavering, you often forget that you can keep that excitement in your heart for God going, no matter what circumstances you find yourself in.

It takes a lot of discipline to keep your hope in God strong. It's something that you have to keep working on every day of your life by reading His word, praying by yourself and with your friends and family, and praising Him no matter what. It is your golden opportunity to tell others who may not know God, about the hope you have inside you. It is your opportunity to tell them how faithful He is. You can tell them how a relationship with the King of Kings can and will change their life if they are willing to let Him into their lives. You can help them know and hold on to true hope.

Prayer of Relief:
Dear Lord, please help me to remember to hold on
to your hope. Help me to lead others to a relationship
with you. Thank you that you're forever faithful.

HOPE IN GOD'S WORD

"I wait for the Lord, my soul waits, and in his word, I hope;"
Psalms 130:5 ESV

Waiting for things in life can be difficult. Waiting can make you impatient and make you start to think that everything has to happen right now. Waiting for the Lord can sometimes be difficult too. You want the answers to your prayers now. But God could be making you stronger and more persistent in your prayers by having you wait.

There is nothing wrong with waiting for some things that you want in your life. The longer you wait for something, most likely, the more thankful you will be when you get it. You can keep your hope and faith in the Lord and His promises whenever you are in a season of waiting. Remind yourself of how He has come through for you in your past and have the faith that He will do it again. Put your hope in His word and remind yourself that His words and promises are as true today as they were more than 2,000 years ago.

Waiting for things will not seem like such a burden if your hope is in God alone. You know that He will "supply all your needs according to His good and gracious will." (Philippians 4:19) He will not let your hope go to waste in any way, and He will reward you for keeping your hope in Him. Instead of looking at waiting as a burden, see it as a privilege and think about all the things you can learn while waiting. Be grateful for the things you learned in that time.

PRAYER FOR COMFORT:
Dear Lord, please help me not grow weary in waiting.
Thank you for all your promises are true.

Rejoice in Hope

"Through him we have also obtained access by faith into this grace in which we stand, and we rejoice in hope of the glory of God."
Romans 5:2 ESV

Try your best to stay happy in every circumstance instead of giving in to the despair that this life can bring you. Ask God to remind you of the hope you have through your relationship with Him. Whenever you're tempted to think about how bad things are in your life, ask God to remind you that you have instant access to Him through prayer. Through faith, you have obtained the ultimate access to God. You can talk to Him at any time, anywhere, no matter how you may be feeling.

Embrace the fact that God loves you enough to give you an all-access pass to Him whenever you want to and need to talk to Him. No one else in your life will ever give you instant access to peace, hope, and love the way God can. No one else in your life is willing to talk to you at a moment's notice or to listen to the cries of your heart the way God is.

Instead of giving into the despair of life, rejoice in the glory of God in your life. You can stand in His grace and glory at any time. There are so many blessings that God has given you. All you have to do is open your heart and mind to receive them. Rejoice in the hope of the glory of your relationship with God.

Prayer for Guidance:
Dear God, whenever I start to complain about life, please
remind me of the hope I have through my relationship with you.
Help me to never take my relationship with you for granted.

INNER SELF RENEWED

"So we do not lose heart. Though our outer self is wasting
away, our inner self is being renewed day by day."
2 Corinthians 4:16 ESV

If you have ever felt overwhelmed about life, you're not the only one. Everyone has felt that sense of dread at one point or another in their life. The good news is that you don't have to lose heart, even if your situation might look hopeless to you. Even when your body is in constant pain, or you just feel like you need an emotional breather, you don't have to lose heart. Even though it seems as though your outer body is wasting away, you aren't wasting away. God is still fulfilling His wonderful plan for your life.

Even though it seems like your outer body can't take the pressures and stresses of your daily life as well as it used to, through your faith in God, your inner spirit is being renewed every day. You can do many things to keep your mind sharp and focused on God. Through daily prayer, devotionals, reading the Bible and spending time at church, and even quiet one on one time with Him in nature, you are renewing your relationship with Him. By doing all of those things, you are making Him a priority in your life. By keeping Him close, you are renewing your spirit every day. Never give up, even when life is hard, because one day, you'll get your reward by being with Jesus in heaven.

PRAYER OF COMFORT:
Dear Lord, please help me to renew my mind by
staying focused on you every day. Help me to
remember that a relationship with you is the most
important relationship I can ever have.

HOPE IS NOT LOST

"Surely there is a future, and your hope will not be cut off."
Proverbs 23:18 ESV

Think back to a time when you thought all hope was lost in your life. Whether it was the death of a family member, a friend, or being diagnosed with an illness yourself, you may have felt like there wasn't any reason to keep hoping. You may have cried out to God in despair and asked Him to end your suffering in ways that only He can. You may have thought your cries landed on deaf ears.

God wants to reassure you today that your cries and prayers have not fallen on deaf ears. He hears every single thing you say and knows every tear that you cry. He wants you to know that He has a future prepared for you, both in heaven and on earth. He has a wonderful plan for your life, and He wants you to succeed and be happy. He wants to hold you in His arms and give you the reassurance that all hope is not lost. You are never cut off from Him or the hope that He gives to you. He wants to hear the cries of your heart and to help you turn your anguish into inexplainable joy. That joy can only come through knowing Him as your heavenly Father. He also wants you to know that He has a place prepared for you in heaven. So even if you've lost hope, rest assured that Jesus hears your cries and is working on helping you overcome your struggles.

PRAYER FOR WORRIED:
Dear God, please heal my pain and calm my anxious
thoughts. Help me to remember that hope isn't
lost because I have a relationship with you.

Rest Securely

*"And you will feel secure, because there is hope;
you will look around and take your rest in security."*
Job 11:18-19 ESV

Whenever there are times when you feel insecure or feel like your life is spiraling out of control, take this scripture and hold it close to your heart. You don't ever need to feel insecure or because you don't do things just like everyone else does. Remember God made you in His image. He gave you unique, special talents that He knew you were going to use.

God wants you to feel secure in your relationship with Him. He wants you to remember that there is always hope and something to look forward to. He wants you to feel the secure hope of the amazing things to come in your future with Him in eternity. So, whenever you are overwhelmed, turn to God in prayer either out loud or in the stillness of your heart and pour out your heart to Him. He longs to talk to you, and He longs to help take your insecurities away. He wants to make you sure of who you are and what you are capable of through Him. He longs to fill you with His peace that surpasses all human understanding. He wants you to rest in His assurance that He has you securely in His arms at all times. He wants you to look around you and rest in the security of His never-ending love.

Prayer for Guidance:
Dear Lord, thank you for reassuring me that there is
hope now and in the future. Thank you for hearing
my prayers. Please help me to focus on you and rest in
your everlasting security when tough times arise.

DEFEND YOUR FAITH

"But in your hearts honor Christ the Lord as holy, always being
prepared to make a defense to anyone who asks you for a reason
for the hope that is in you; yet do it with gentleness and respect."
1 Peter 3:15 ESV

Have you ever had anyone ask you how you go through life with so much hope in your heart? Are you prepared to give them an answer about the hope that you get from having a relationship with Jesus? What would you say to someone who asked you about those things?

You can tell them something like this: "God helped me change my life around for the better. He saved my life in more ways than one. Having a relationship with Him is the best thing I have ever done in my life." Then you can give them some specific ways He helped you in your life and say something like: "God can help you have the hope in your heart that you long for too. He is the reason why I have hope in my life. I know that no matter what happens, Jesus has everything under control. He can and will see you through hard times in your life too."

Instead of getting defensive when someone asks about the hope you have, you can see it as one of the greatest opportunities to tell that person about God. It allows you to pray for, and with the person you're talking to. Be gracious and answer their questions with respect.

PRAYER FOR GUIDANCE:
Dear God, please help me share the hope I have
with others. Thank you for allowing me to share
the hope I have gained through knowing you.

Revelation of Jesus' Coming

"Therefore, preparing your minds for action, and being sober-minded, set your hope fully on the grace that will be brought to you at the revelation of Jesus Christ."
1 Peter 1:13 ESV

You might be asking yourself how you can prepare your mind for the action of Jesus' return. All you have to do is be alert at all times and keep your focus on God as much as you possibly can. The reason for keeping your mind alert is because only God Himself knows the day and time He will have Jesus' return to take all believers to heaven. Set your hope fully on the grace that will be bestowed on you at Jesus' second coming. If you love God with all your heart, you will have the reward of being in heaven for all eternity with Him.

You can be prepared for action by reading God's word and reading devotionals every day to get closer to God. No matter how hard things can get in your life, you can rest assured in the promise of the hope that God freely gives to you through faith in Jesus. You don't have to fear death as the non-believers might because you know that Jesus has a place prepared for you in heaven. Instead of focusing on the hardships of life, remember that you already have your reward lined up when you get to heaven. You may lose battles, but take courage and remember that Jesus has already won the war against Satan and death on the cross.

PRAYER FOR RELIEF:
Dear Lord, please help me to stay focused on you throughout my life. Help me to set my mind on the hope that only comes from you. Thank you for giving me victory over every obstacle.

WORK OF FAITH

"Remembering before our God and Father your work of faith and labor of love and steadfastness of hope in our Lord Jesus Christ."
1 Thessalonians 1:3 ESV

Some days in your life can seem more like burdens instead of joyous occasions. It takes much work, dedication, grit, and willpower to keep your mind focused on God at all times. It isn't something that you just learn to do overnight either. It is a lifelong process that you have to work on getting more proficient at every day of your life. Before you start telling yourself that you will never learn everything you need to know about God, remember that God doesn't want you to know everything. You don't have to be so hard on yourself. God doesn't look down on you for not knowing everything in life. God knows that you'll stumble and fall in your labor of love towards Him. He doesn't expect you to get everything exactly right. He won't punish you for doing things wrong either.

He wants you to find the littlest joy in every day, no matter how crazy this life gets for you. He wants you to seek Him out. He wants you to let the hope of Jesus come into your heart and flood your soul with peace like a warm blanket. He will reward you for your works of faith, the labor of love, and your steadfast hope in Jesus.

PRAYER FOR WORRIED:
Dear God, please help me to see the joys in life instead of
the burdens. Please help me to keep my faith in you strong
in every way possible. When things in life are difficult,
help me to remember the hope I have through you.

Greatness Among Us

"To them God chose to make known how great among
the Gentiles are the riches of the glory of this mystery,
which is Christ in you, the hope of glory."
Colossians 1:27 ESV

God wants to display His greatness among us in every way possible. It is the same way He wanted to show His greatness to the people in biblical times. He wanted to share the riches of His glory to everyone that would listen to His message through His Son Jesus. He wants everyone to know how great He is in every way possible. You and other people might be wondering what some of the riches of God are. You can help people understand what the glory and the mystery of God is, within your heart.

All you have to do is explain to them who God is to you and how He has changed your life. You can explain how He has helped you through many hard times. If they have questions about God, be willing to answer them in any way you can. If you can't answer their questions, point them to someone like a pastor.

Be bold and talk about your faith in front of your friends and family without worrying if they'll judge you for talking about Him. Boldly proclaim your love for Him, the same way Jesus proclaimed His love for His Father. God chose to make His greatness known among the Gentiles. Be brave enough to make Him known throughout your life.

Prayer for Help:
Dear Lord, please help me to be bold enough to tell
others about you. Help me to want to tell others about
you. Thank you for the opportunity to declare your
goodness and mercy all the days of my life.

Don't Live with Grief

"…And do not be grieved, for the joy of the Lord is your strength."
Nehemiah 8:10 ESV

It is ok to be sad when things don't go your way in life. It's ok to feel discouraged when things aren't working out. But it's important not to stay in that place of sadness forever. You don't have to be grieved and angry until things start to work out. Instead, you can still find joy in your struggles. Look for the silver linings of God's favor in your life. Things such as the crispness of the autumn air or the color of the leaves in the fall. Other things to notice are the ability to see and hear the birds chirping, the ability to see a beautiful sunset when God knows you need it the most. You have the privilege to come before God and tell Him exactly how you feel at any moment.

He wants you to have joy knowing that you have a relationship with Him. He also wants you to rely on Him for strength when it feels like you can't take another step. He will carry you through hard times when it seems you've lost all hope. Instead of thinking things can't get any worse, remember that God can change any situation around. Remember how He carried you through difficult circumstances before, and He will do it again. Find joy in your life that can only come through a relationship with Him.

Prayer for Comfort:
Dear God, please help me to not live with grief despite hard circumstances. Help me to see your goodness every day. Help me to focus on you in everything I do. Thank you for always being my joy and for being here for me no matter what.

FEAR OF GOD

"Is not your fear of God your confidence,
and the integrity of your ways your hope?"
Job 4:6 ESV

Having a fear of God can make people confused. Most people think that having a fear of someone or something means that you're afraid of something or someone. On the contrary, being fearful of something means that you have a healthy respect for it and that you are aware of it. Being fearful of God doesn't mean that you're afraid of Him. It means that you know Him and that you have both great respect and knowledge of Him.

This scripture goes into further detail, asking you if your healthy "fear" and knowledge of God can be your confidence. Think about it for a second. Do you want your fear of God to be your confidence? Do you want the integrity and the relationship that you have with God to be your hope? If your answer is yes, you have to make your relationship with God an even bigger priority than what it used to be. There is nothing wrong with making God the most important person in your life right here, right now.

Let your wonder about God become your thirst for knowledge about Him. Let your intimidations about God be your main talking points to Him in prayer. Ask Him to reveal things to you about His character in ways that only He can. Turn your intimidation of Him into the confidence that you have always longed for. Let the integrity of His ways be your hope.

PRAYER FOR GUIDANCE:
Dear God, please help me change my mindset of you from intimidation to awe and wonder. Reveal things about yourself to me that I never expected to learn. Help me to want to know you more.

FULFIL PRAYER REQUESTS

"Oh that I might have my request,
and that God would fulfill my hope…"
Job 6:8 ESV

It is completely ok to put everything on the table and to present your requests to God at any time. No matter how you may be feeling, you can always come to God in prayer and tell Him how you feel. He encourages you to come to Him and tell Him what you are going through, how you are feeling, and what your needs are, even though He knows all of that information already. He wants to have an intimate relationship with you, no matter how far you may have strayed from Him. He sees you losing your way and your hope, and He wants to give you your reassurance, clarity, and peace of mind back.

You don't have to ever be afraid to come to Him in prayer. He wants you to be sure in your relationship with Him so much that you boldly ask Him for things in your life that other people may not ask for. He wants to be your everlasting hope in times of trouble, uncertainty, and in times of pain. He wants to fulfill your wishes, dreams, desires and hopes in ways that you can't even imagine. All you have to do is ask Him to be with you and to fill your soul with the peace and hope that can only come from Him. Then you will see Him move in mighty ways throughout your life.

PRAYER OF GRATITUDE:
Dear God, help me to boldly come before you in prayer. Help me not be afraid to ask you anything or to tell you exactly what I need. Thank you for fulfilling my hope in every way possible.

Hope in His Love

*"But the Lord takes pleasure in those who fear him,
in those who hope in his steadfast love."*
Psalm 147:11 ESV

The Lord loves everyone, including those who choose not to know Him and those who choose to know Him. But the Lord has taken pleasure in those who have a serious relationship with Him. Those who have hope in His steadfast love will never be put to shame by Him. God wants everyone to know Him and to have a personal relationship with Him.

So, if you think that you've lost all hope or that you can't ever get back on track with God, think again. If you've been fed that lie that God doesn't love you because of your mistakes, think again. If you think there is no way that God would accept you back as His child, stop thinking like that. God loves you despite your sins and your mistakes. God loves you no matter what you have done.

If you want to get back on track with God, you have every opportunity to do it now. Read your Bible again, start praying, even if it's small prayers. Don't count yourself down and out because God still wants you to return to Him as His child. He loves you no matter what you have done. He wants you to hope in Him and to have the reassurance that He will work out all things for your good. He has always been there for you, and He will continue to be there for you, even when you feel as though you don't deserve a relationship with Him.

Prayer of Relief:
Dear God, please help me remember that no
matter what I've done I can have a relationship
with you. Thank you for always pursuing me.

GOD IS YOUR PORTION

"The Lord is my portion," says my soul,
"therefore I will hope in him."
Lamentations 3:24 ESV

The Lord can be your portion if you only let Him. He can be your stronghold in times of uncertainty, your rock in hard times, and your anchor to cling to in the middle of life's devastating storms. He can be your portion forever that floods your mind with peace. Instead of giving into the fear that life gives you, you can cling to the hope that Jesus freely gives you. When others see you holding on to hope when they think you should be completely falling apart, you can explain that even though hard times have come upon you, you have no reason to fear. They might look at you like you are crazy when you tell them that you have every reason to continue to hope for the great things to come in your life. It is ok if people don't understand where your hope comes from. They might even be all the more curious about the way you live your life.

You can gladly tell them that your hope doesn't come from this world, but it comes from knowing that God's always with you. Your hope comes from having a relationship with Jesus. You can tell them that they can have the same hope you have if they want to know God. It allows you to witness those people and help them understand the hope that they are missing out on.

PRAYER FOR GUIDANCE:
Dear Lord, please help me to have continual hope in you, despite life's circumstances. Help me to continue to shine your light in life. Thank you for being my source of everlasting hope.

Purified from Sin

"And everyone who thus hopes in him purifies himself as he is pure."
1 John 3:3 ESV

When you have hope in God who is eternal, you know that your soul will find eternal rest once you get to heaven. This scripture says everyone that hopes in Him is purified as God is pure. God knows that you fall short of the mark every single day. But He gives His grace, mercy, peace, unending forgiveness, and love to you and everyone that calls on His name.

You are purified through Him and your relationship with Him. Embrace the purity that you have from God and do your best not to sin every day. Even when it seems as though your sins are too big to forgive or that God won't love you because of one specific sin, God still loves you and wants to give you His unending forgiveness. Thank Him that He can turn your messes into masterpieces. Thank God that He can turn any test into a testimony that you can share with the world.

God can and will purify you until you shine bright like the sun and shimmer white like the snowflakes. He wants you to embrace the purity that you can only find in your relationship with Him. He wants you to have the hope that you can only have from knowing Him. Remember how He brought you out of the mud and mire into the place of light that you're in now. Take time to thank Him for His redeeming love.

Prayer for Help:
Dear Lord, thank you for making me clean and for
giving me purity from my sin. Help me to want to
stay pure in my relationship with you. Thank you
for turning my mess into a masterpiece.

HOPE IS NOT CRUSHED

"But the needy will not be ignored forever;
the hopes of the poor will not always be crushed."
Psalm 9:18 NLT

When was the last time you felt like you were in need or want of something? Have you ever wondered how your needs would be met? God will always supply your needs no matter what you ask Him for. If you are in need, go to God in prayer and put your requests before Him. If you have lost hope, you can ask Him to fill your heart with the hope that He will take care of you. If you feel God is ignoring you, remember, He sees and knows you better than anyone else does. He knew you before you were even born. He will not leave you out to dry. You will be let down by people on earth, but He will never let you down.

If you have ever encountered someone that has lost hope in their time of need, you can be an encouragement to them. If you have ever met a poor person, give them what little you have. Tell them about Jesus and the hope He has to offer them. They will not always have their hope crushed, and neither will you. God will be your everlasting hope and provide ways around and over any obstacle in your path. Give thanks to Him that He sees your needs and the needs of others around you. Look around you. Ask God how you can be a blessing to someone else who needs something more than you.

PRAYER FOR GUIDANCE:
Dear Lord, thank you that I can be a blessing to someone else.
Please help me to look at the needs of those around me.

God's Unfailing Love

"Let your unfailing love surround us,
LORD, for our hope is in you alone."
Psalm 33:22 NLT

If you have ever felt like all hope was lost, you're not the only one. Everyone goes through times of hopelessness in their life, and they might think that there is no way out. On the contrary, there are ways out of every situation through knowing God. Trusting in God to be your hope is one of the best things you can do. God's love is never-ending, inexplicable, and never failing. All you have to do to experience it is call on His name. His unfailing love surrounds you at every single stage of your life. Whether you are a brand-new believer or have known God since you were a kid, His love is all around you. No matter how far you wander from Him, He is never far from you. He wants you to trust in His beautiful plan for your life and know that everything will turn out ok.

He has you in the palm of His hands and wants to give you hope that can be felt despite your circumstances. He wants you to hold on to His everlasting hope. He doesn't want you to ever give up on yourself because He will never give up on you. He wants you to be confident, knowing His unfailing love is always with you. Pray that you feel His presence in everything you do and in everything you think. Ask Him to reveal different ways to get to know Him better in every area of your life.

PRAYER OF HELP:
Dear Lord, thank you for being my source of
everlasting hope. Thank you for never giving up
on me, even when I give up on myself.

GOD WILL SAVE YOU

"As for me, I look to the Lord for help. I wait confidently
for God to save me and my God will certainly hear me."
Micah 7:7 NLT

There's nothing wrong with asking God for help with your problems. He's the one you should automatically turn to when you're facing a problem. You shouldn't vent to your friends or family because all that will make you feel worse about your situation. On the other hand, praying about your problems gives you more clarity to think things through and more peace of mind. Praying takes your focus off the problem to the One who can fix the problem. Instead of focusing on how big your problems are, remind yourself that God has gotten you through rough times before. Remember how amazed you were every time He came through for you.

That way, when someone asks you how you handle your problems, no matter how big or small they are, you can confidently say that your most productive weapon is prayer. You can have the confidence that He hears your prayers no matter how you say them, whether you pray alone or with a group. You know without a shadow of a doubt that God hears you whenever you pray and that He will deliver you. He has done it before, and He will certainly do it again. If you make a habit of coming to Jesus first whenever a problem arises, it will become easier to come to Him no matter what happens to you.

PRAYER FOR WORRIED:
Lord Jesus, thank you for always hearing my prayers
and for delivering me from hard times. Help me
remember to come to you first whenever I have a
problem, instead of telling my problems to others.

Let God Lead Your Life

"Lead me by your truth and teach me, for you are the
God who saves me. All day long I put my hope in you."
Psalm 25:5 NLT

Who are you being led by? Are you being led by yourself and your ambitions? Are you being led by the world and what everyone else in the world wants to teach you? Or are you being led by God and listening to what He wants to teach you throughout your life? The most important person to listen to is God Himself. He knows that you will get led astray by the world and everything the world throws at you. But He wants you to listen to His truth instead of giving into the lies that this world throws at you.

He wants you to cling to the truth of His word every day of your life. God wants you to be led by His truth and to learn from Him in every way possible. His ways are infinitely better than yours, and no one will ever love you more than God Himself. Ask Him to show you the mystery and wonder of the world through His eyes. Ask Him to put the awe into your heart about the beauty of the world around you. He can teach you things that you never expected to know. Let His word make you want to know more and more about Him every day. He will lead you in your life as long as you give Him the opportunity to do so. If you let Him lead you, you'll experience more joy and happiness than you ever thought possible.

Prayer for Guidance:
Dear Lord, please take over my life. Lead me
in your ways and teach me your truth.

GLORIOUS HOPE

"For there is one body and one Spirit, just as you have been called to one glorious hope for the future."
Ephesians 4:4 NLT

No matter how hard things can and will get for you in your life, if you have the hope of the Lord in your life, you can always have hope for the future. No matter how bleak things seem, with God on your side, you can and will get through anything. As a believer, you are called to the glorious hope through Jesus. He gives you the power to believe in the hope for your future. There is nothing you can't get through with God at your side. You can become one with Jesus in your body and your spirit. There are many ways in which you can get close to God.

You can get close to Him physically by reading His word or by reading devotionals every day. You can also get close to Him physically by going to church every week and by interacting with other believers in the church. By viewing every day as a blessing, you can begin to see blessings pop up from anywhere, and you will point them out to your family and friends. You will realize that there is always something to be happy, hopeful, and grateful for. You will tend to see blessings in every situation instead of burdens.

You can become close to Him physically, mentally, and spiritually by praying about anything and everything in your life. You can cling to the hope He gives you and look forward to a glorious future.

PRAYER FOR COMFORT:
Dear Lord, please help me to get closer to you in
any way possible. Thank you for the opportunity
to have a glorious future because of you.

Be Glad and Rejoice

"I know the Lord is always with me. I will not be shaken,
for he is right beside me. No wonder my heart is glad,
and I rejoice. My body rests in safety."
Psalm 16:8-9 NLT

Have you taught yourself to be glad no matter the circumstances that come your way? Do you feel God right beside you when things start to get tough, or do you sink away into the deep corners of your mind wondering how you will get through the next obstacle? You don't have to fear what will come next in your life because God is always with you. He is there to help you whenever you call on Him. You can rest assured that He wants what is best for you and that He is moving mountains on your behalf.

Whenever things become too hard to handle, you can shift your focus from your problems to the One who can and will get you through them. Instead of saying things like, "there's no way I'll get through this," or, "this is too difficult for me," or, "I'm not a good fit for this position at work," start saying positive things to reaffirm your hope in God. Start saying things like, "I know God is with me. He has me in the palm of His hands. He won't let me fall." "I won't fear the unknown because God is already there."

When you start rejoicing and keeping your heart glad, you will feel more at peace and more at rest. Remember, God wants you to be happy at all times.

PRAYER FOR WORRIED:
Dear God, please help me to turn to you in uncertain
times. Help me to enjoy my life. Thank you that
you are always with me in every situation.

You Aren't Helpless

"Lord, you know the hopes of the helpless.
Surely you will hear their cries and comfort them."
Psalm 10:17 NLT

Being hopeless is difficult. It can break you down and bring you into the pits of utter despair if you aren't careful. The good news is that you have a best friend in your life that already knows whenever you feel helpless and hopeless. His name is Jesus. He knows how you are feeling and how you are struggling before you even begin to struggle. He knows how you will think there is no way you can get through the obstacles in your path. The great news is that He already has solutions lined up for your problem. He had the solutions lined up for you, way before your problems even began. If God knew your problems and how they would affect you, take courage in knowing that He already knows just how to help you through them. There is nothing that He hasn't already seen in your past, present, or your future, that will ever make Him decide to turn His back on you.

He hears the cries of your heart and wants to comfort you with His peace. He longs to embrace you with His loving arms and to tell you that everything will be alright. In His eyes, you are not helpless. You are more than a conqueror. You are a victor, even in the smallest sense. Let His comfort come over you like a warm blanket. Rest in the assurance that He will always help you.

Prayer for Comfort:
Dear Lord, please help me to remember that you are
helping me, even when things seem helpless in my life.
Thank you for being my ultimate source of comfort.

RIGHTEOUSNESS OF GOD

*"But we who live by the Spirit eagerly wait to receive
by faith the righteousness God has promised to us."*
Galatians 5:5 NLT

There are many ways in which you can live by the Holy Spirit. You can live by the spirit by filling your mind with life-affirming sayings every single day. Whenever you are tempted to say something negative, ask God to help you take that negativity and turn it into a positive thought about yourself. Whenever you are tempted to think badly about another person, ask God to help change your view of them. Whenever a task seems too big to handle, take a moment to catch your breath and refocus your thoughts. Tell yourself that God wouldn't place this task in front of you if He didn't think you were capable of completing it.

God has promised to make you righteous in His sight, and He has done just that. He sees you as His beloved child who is more than a conqueror and more than capable of completing seemingly impossible tasks. You are allowed to live by the spirit and in the spirit every day. Since you are a believer, you already have the righteousness of God within you. All you have to do is apply it to your everyday life situations. If you live by the spirit, you will continually obtain the righteousness of God. God has promised to be with you in every situation, and He will give you the hope that you need in your heart and your life whenever you ask Him for it.

PRAYER FOR GUIDANCE:
Dear Lord, please help me receive the righteousness
of faith by calling on your name every day. Thank
you for helping me strengthen my faith.

HOPEFUL IN GOD

*"But joyful are those who have the God of Israel as
their helper, whose hope is in the Lord their God."*
Psalm 146:5 NLT

You might be in a place right now where you are wondering when your joy will return. You might be asking yourself, "how can I possibly have any hope when my life is falling apart?" Instead of being miserable when life doesn't work out the way you want it to, start asking God to fill you with the joy that is inexplainable, the joy that you can only experience through a close relationship with Him.

The Bible says people are joyful when they have God as their helper. It also says people are more joyful when they know they have everlasting hope in God. When you start thinking negatively, God can help you turn that negative thinking around and help you start thinking positively. When you realize that you can call upon God any time you need help, that's when you know you have the source of everlasting power in your life. There is nothing God won't do for you. He can make ways where there seems to be no way.

You can strengthen your hope in God throughout your life by reading your Bible, going to church every week, and praying even in those moments where you just don't feel like it. Often when you least want to pray about things, that is when He reveals things to you that you hadn't realized you needed to know.

PRAYER OF GRATITUDE:
Dear God, please help me to see you as my ultimate source
of help in everyday life. Thank you that I can call on you
at any time. Thank you for always being here for me.

You Can!

"What do you mean, 'If I can'?" Jesus asked.
"Anything is possible if a person believes."
Mark 9:23 NLT

There have probably been many times where you've been close to giving up all hope. You have second-guessed your abilities to work, to lead projects, to help your family have a closer relationship with God, to make your marriage work, to spend more time with your friends. The list of ways that you can second guess yourself goes on and on. You have the power of life and death in your own words, actions, and your thoughts. What you think will become what you say. What you say will become what you do.

Instead of second-guessing yourself and thinking things like "I don't know if I can do (name obstacle)," or "I can't do this," or "I don't think I can do this," remind yourself that you have the power of God within you at all times. He is just waiting for you to start saying powerful, uplifting statements about yourself. He wants you to remember that you can do all things through Him, who gives you strength. (Philippians 4:13). The next time you have a hard task in front of you, instead of talking yourself into not being able to do it, say, "I know I can do this because nothing is impossible with God. God is on my side, and I know He will help me." All you have to do is believe that God gave you the ability to do the task in front of you.

Prayer for Help:
Dear Lord, please help me believe that I can do
anything you have set in front of me. Thank you
for helping me see your strength within me.

Don't Trust in Money

"Teach those who are rich in this world not to be proud and not to trust in their money, which is so unreliable. Their trust should be in God, who richly gives us all we need for our enjoyment."
1 Timothy 6:17 NLT

You probably have thought, "If I could only have more money. Then things would be better for me in my life." That isn't the right attitude to have. You should be able to look at your life and see the blessings you have right now without thinking about money.

If you start naming the blessings that you have in your life, you can help others start to be grateful for the blessings they have. You can teach those who are rich not to be too proud of their wealth. You can advise them not to trust in their money or to put too much of their hope in their money. Trusting and hoping in money can only lead to their ruin. Money is so unreliable because it will eventually run out.

But God's love, grace, and mercy will never run out. He will supply everything that you need to support your body and life. He gives you everything you could want and more. He gives you everything you need for your enjoyment. Take the time to appreciate the little things in life today because they will eventually be the big things you will remember long into the future. Don't always think about how you will make money. Rather, be grateful for the many things God has given you to enjoy.

Prayer for Guidance:
Dear Lord, please help me to trust in you, not in money.
Help me to enjoy every day of my life as a gift from you.

Eternal Hope

*"I am worn out waiting for your rescue,
but I have put my hope in your word."
Psalm 119:81 NLT*

Just like everyone else in this world, you get tired of waiting for things to get better in your life. When things are spiraling out of control, you get mentally, physically, and even spiritually exhausted. Come before God and admit that you are feeling worn out in many different ways. He already knows what will wear you out and why you are worn out. But He is working behind the scenes on your behalf every day.

When you put your hope in God, you are saying to your problems, "I know God will help get me through these things. I know God is in control. I have everlasting assurance from Him." Instead of stressing out, you can turn to God in prayer, asking Him for guidance in each step of your day. You can ask Him for guidance in every decision you make throughout your week. Instead of complaining about your life, you can make lists of the things that you're grateful for, and you can make lists of the things that are going well for you at the moment. Instead of dreading the future, you can look towards the future with optimism. With God's help, you can stay positive even in difficult times. You go to sleep at night in peace, no matter how chaotic your day might have been. Trusting in Him is something you have to work on daily, but the rewards you will reap are everlasting.

Prayer of Comfort:
Dear Lord, thank you for the privilege to see the world
through your eyes. Thank you that I can put my hope
in you, no matter how my day might be going.

TRUE HAPPINESS

*"The hopes of the godly result in happiness,
but the expectations of the wicked come to nothing."*
Proverbs 10:28 NLT

When you have hope in God, it doesn't mean things are just automatically going to be easy for you. On the contrary. Things can sometimes be harder for you when you start to trust God. That's because Satan doesn't want you to trust God in everything that you do. Satan doesn't want you to have joy or hope in your life. He wants to keep you stressed out and joyless. It makes him mad when you turn your worries over to God instead of letting them build up. He wants you to keep being stressed out, so you don't feel mentally or physically capable of the things that God wants you to do.

But God wants you to seek His Son Jesus and ask Him for the joy that can only be found with having a relationship with Him. He wants to take away the stress of this world that Satan puts on your shoulders. God is saying to you, "Hey, I'm right here. If you're feeling like the weight of the world is on you, come to me, and I'll gladly take the burden off of your shoulders. Let me carry it for you."

Those people who carry the hope of God in their hearts have much more happiness, but the expectations of the wicked will never come to know the true peace of God. The true peace of God comes from knowing that your happiness doesn't come from the world. It comes from knowing that Jesus is the source of your happiness.

PRAYER FOR GUIDANCE:
Dear God, please help me remember that my true
happiness comes from you, not this world.

Unfailing Love

"O Israel, hope in the Lord, for with the Lord there
is unfailing love. His redemption overflows."
Psalm 130:7 NLT

True everlasting hope comes from having a personal relationship with God. It is how you can have true happiness in your life, despite the difficulties that life can throw at you. You can have true everlasting hope by hoping in God, even when the world gives you every reason to give up all hope. When you are close to giving up hope and throwing up your hands, saying, "I give up," that is when God whispers in your ear, "My child, try again. This time with me at your side. I will help you and guide you in every decision that you make. Just call on me. I'm here for you." With God, there is unfailing love that will never be taken away from you. No matter how much you may have felt like you have messed up in your life, God still loves you.

He wants you to remember that His love for you extends past the ends of the earth. His redemption overflows from generation to generation. He wants you to remember His love and to embrace His love in every area of your life. When you feel stressed, come to Him in prayer. Tell Him how you are struggling. If you feel lonely, ask Him to send special friends or family members your way to brighten up your life. When you feel unlovable, ask Him to remind you that you are His beloved child. When you feel you've sinned too much, ask Him for forgiveness.

PRAYER OF RELIEF:
Dear God, please help me to remember that
through you, I have everlasting love. Thank you
that I can have hope in you no matter what.

TRUSTING GOD

*"Through Christ, you have come to trust in God.
And you have placed your faith and hope in God because
he raised Christ from the dead and gave him great glory."*
1 Peter 1:21 NLT

How old were you when you came to know Christ as your Savior? Can you say that you fully trust Him? Or is having complete trust in Him something that you're struggling with? Trusting God comes with knowing that through Him, you can and will get through any obstacles that come your way. You know that God will see you through to the other side no matter what happens in your life.

There is nothing wrong with sometimes questioning God and questioning your faith. God wants you to ask questions about your faith and ask questions about Him. God sent Jesus to die for you on the cross to cover your sins and the sins of everyone else on earth. He loved you so much that He gave His one and only Son up to die on the cross to take away your sins. Then after three days, God raised Jesus from the dead and gave Him great glory. He is preparing a great place for you in heaven. Placing your faith and hope in Him means that you trust Him to help you in every area of your life. You can go about your days in peace because you know God already has a solution to the problem you're facing. Even when life gets you down, remember the price Jesus paid for you. Remember that you have the hope of heaven waiting for you.

PRAYER OF GRATITUDE:
Dear Lord, thank you for raising Jesus to glory and
for giving me a place in heaven with Him.

Put Hope in God's Word

"You are my shelter and my shield. I put my hope in your word."
Psalm 119:114 CSB

Whenever you are tempted to think negatively, you can change your thinking around. All you have to do is ask God to change your thinking into something constructive instead of destructive. Be forewarned, though; it isn't something that you just learn overnight. It is something that you have to learn throughout your whole life. God can and will help you turn any negative thoughts into positive ones. Tell yourself, "God is my shield. He is my shelter. I can trust in Him at all times. I can put my hope in His word." You can teach yourself to turn negative thoughts into positive thoughts. Whenever a negative thought enters your mind, you can learn to say positive things instead.

When you think about getting strength from God or the world, sometimes you go for the outer strength of the world. The world will fail to give you strength every time. But instead of turning to the world for strength, you can turn to God for strength. He has the strength to get you through any and every situation.

When you're tempted to give in to negative thoughts, you can say, "I know God will get me through this." "I can put His word into my heart, and I know He can help me through anything." "The Lord is the source of my strength. He is the source of my peace. He gives me hope even in difficult situations." "He has never failed me, and He never will."

Turn to Him for shelter and strength. Ask Him to be the safe place that you can always turn to. Ask Him for the strength you need, and He will strengthen you in ways you never thought possible. You will feel empowered and ready to take on anything that comes your way.

Prayer for Worried:
Dear Lord, please help me to turn to you instead of turning
to the world for strength. Thank you that you will never
fail me. Thank you for being my shelter in hard times
and for reminding me to put my hope in your word.

TRUST IN THE LORD

*"The person who trusts in the Lord,
whose confidence indeed is the Lord, is blessed."*
Jeremiah 17:7 CSB

Isn't it a relief to know that if you trust in the Lord, He will bless you? Think about that for a second. You will be blessed when you trust in the Lord. That means instead of walking around being miserable in every circumstance, you can walk around with God's word firmly in your heart. Instead of walking around thinking how things will never change or get any better for you, you can walk around with the confidence of knowing that God is with you. You can be confident and have hope in your heart, no matter what goes on in life.

Instead of giving in to the negative self-pity talk of, "why do all the bad things happen to me? Why can't I catch a break?" you can change your thoughts around and say, "despite how difficult things are right now, I choose to have the hope of God in me. I am not going to let the little things become big things and let them drag me down. I know God has a plan and a purpose for my life. Instead of being hopeless, I will remain hopeful that the best days of my life are yet to come."

When you have the hope of God residing in you, your heart, mind, and your life will be filled with peace. Wouldn't you love to have more confidence in your life? Now you can put those thoughts into words and actions every day. Choose to trust Him and put your hope in Him. There is no one better and no one greater to put your hope and trust in than God Himself. When you trust Him, you will be blessed in more ways than you can possibly imagine. Choose to make your life better today.

PRAYER FOR COMFORT:

Dear God, please help me to learn to trust you more and more
every day. Thank you that you are my source of everlasting
peace and hope. Thank you for blessing me with more
clarity and peace of mind. Thank you for the confidence
that I can have through my relationship with you.

Faith in His Name

"And his name—by faith in his name—has made this man strong
whom you see and know, and the faith that is through Jesus has
given the man this perfect health in the presence of you all."
Acts 3:16 ESV

If you have ever gone through any sickness, often, your first prayer and wish
is to be completely healed. It is not fun being sick at all. Nor is it fun to
deal with other ailments such as blindness, crippling chronic pain, or can-
cer. In this Scripture, there was a man that was lame (unable to walk) from
birth. He was at the entrance to the gate of the church where Jesus' disci-
ples Peter and John were entering. He was begging for money. They told
him they didn't have any silver or gold to give him, but for him to get up
and walk in the name of Jesus. At once, his legs were strengthened, and he
could walk for the first time in his life. His faith in Jesus allowed him to do
an amazing thing in front of many witnesses. Your faith in Jesus can help
you accomplish many amazing things too.

Your faith can restore you to perfect health, just like this man's faith restored
him to health and allowed him to be able to walk. Your faith can help you
through anything that seems impossible. If you have ever seen the miracle of
someone being healed or even had that miracle happen to you, you know what
it is like to be leaping for joy, praising God the way this man was. Whenever
God brings you healing, let it strengthen your faith. Jesus brings you healing so
you can become even closer to Him. His healing gives you the ability to share
the good news of Jesus with everyone around you. Praise Him with everything
you have. If He can bring instant healing to the lame man, imagine all of the
amazing things He can do for you in your life.

Prayer for Worried:
Dear God, please help me and bring me healing. Help me
to know that my faith can help me do miraculous things.

God Rejoices Over You

*"The Lord your God is among you, a warrior who saves.
He will rejoice over you with gladness. He will be quiet
in his love. He will delight in you with singing."*
Zephaniah 3:17 CSB

God is a warrior who can and will save you from any adversity if you only let Him. He doesn't want to see you struggling in your life. Whenever you set your hope in Him, He rejoices over you with gladness. He rejoices every time you come back to Him, asking for forgiveness for the things you have done wrong. He smiles every time you call on His name, whether it is because you have a prayer request, are interceding on your family or friend's behalf, or you want to praise Him in worship. He loves when you talk to Him. He loves it when you make time to read His word. He is a warrior who will move in mighty ways for you. He will be quiet in His love for you. He will never force His love on you, but as you go through life, you will see His love in ways that you never expected.

He will never force you to follow Him, but you can choose to follow Him. He wants you to choose to know Him. Once you choose to follow Him, you will gain so much. God will rejoice over you with songs. He and His angels rejoice every time you or someone in your life choose to follow Him. You will know what it's like to have peace, understanding, love, and courage. You will know what it's like to be able to be a witness for Him through to the next generation. You have the opportunity to be a witness for Him every day of your life. You can help those around you know what it's like to have God in their lives. Whenever you have the opportunity to bring someone to Christ, take that opportunity.

PRAYER OF RELIEF:
Dear Lord, thank you for being a mighty warrior
in my life. Thank you for rejoicing in me and for
helping me be a witness to others in my life.

The Armor of Faith

"But since we belong to the day, let us be self-controlled and put on the armor of faith and love, and a helmet of the hope of salvation."
1 Thessalonians 5:8 CSB

It can feel as though this world is overwhelming you with its messages, cultural guidelines, and when people tell you that you should be doing things to their standards. You can often be reminded to have self-control in every situation. Self-control takes discipline every day, and it is something that you have to work on—being self-controlled means not going off in anger whenever someone tries to give you criticism and not getting mad whenever someone tells you something that you don't want to hear.

You can respond in love even when you don't want to. You can put on the full armor of faith and love. This means keeping the faith when the world is telling you to give up faith. It means keeping the hope in your heart when the world screams at you to give up hope. God is saying to you, "keep trying. This time with me. Don't give up just because things become difficult. You are my child, and I love you." Putting on the full armor of faith also means letting yourself know that you are more than a conqueror through Jesus. Jesus wants to bestow His power in your life.

You can also put on the full helmet of the hope of salvation. That means that even when you feel like giving up, you know deep in your soul and mind that you have to keep going. When you persevere through difficulties, you will feel hope rise in your heart, and you will be proud of yourself for making it through things you weren't sure you could get through. The hope of salvation can be the very thing that carries you through every situation in your life.

Prayer for Guidance:
Dear God, please help me always wear the full armor of
faith and love in every battle I face. Help me to remember
to also wear the helmet of the hope of your salvation.

Hope of Eternal Life

*"...in the hope of eternal life that God,
who cannot lie, promised before time began."*
Titus 1:2 CSB

If you've ever thought that there is no hope left for you, remember that God loves you. He only wants what is best for you. He wants you to be full of hope for your future and the things ahead of you. If you have ever thought that there was no possible way out of the struggles that you're in, think again. If you know God, you have the hope of eternal life already dwelling inside you. You have the hope of God living within you at all times. He takes care of you at all times, loves you, and wants to only give you the best life possible.

He wants you to enjoy your life on earth until you get to heaven. He wants you to remember that you have the hope of eternal life waiting for you. Let that thought excite you. You don't have to fear death anymore! You have an eternal place in heaven waiting for you. When you die, you're being received into God's loving arms for all eternity. You will get to see your loved ones again at heaven's gates. Think about it- no matter what battles you face in your life, you can rest assured that Jesus has already won the war over Satan and death by dying on the cross. Let that awesome thought give you peace of mind and rest. Whenever things seem difficult for you to overcome, turn to Jesus to refill your life with the hope that your soul desperately needs. God can not lie, so you know that He's always telling the truth. His word and promises are all true. He promises to supply all your needs. Do everything by His power and in His name. He will give you the hope that you need in your heart. His hope will carry you throughout your life.

PRAYER FOR COMFORT:
Dear Lord, thank you for giving me the hope of eternal life through knowing you. Help me to rely on the hope you give me each day.

There's Hope for You

"There is hope for a tree: If it is cut down, it will sprout again, and its shoots will not die. 8 If its roots grow old in the ground and its stump starts to die in the soil,9 the scent of water makes it thrive and produce twigs like a sapling."
Job 14:7-9 CSB

Hope is the thing that can carry you in life. It gives you the reason to keep going even when you think you can't take another step. It whispers, "try again," even when you have failed for the 100th time at something you're trying your best at. This scripture says if a tree is cut down, it will sprout again, and the roots will not die. The same thing goes for you as a believer in Christ. Whenever someone cuts you down in your life, you do not have to give in to the despair that your life will not get any better. If you make mistakes in your life, which you will, you don't have to fear that no one will ever look at you as a successful person. You can try again at any time throughout your life, with God at your side.

If you are down, you can rise again with God's help. He will give you the strength and perseverance to try again. You will spread your wings and fly again. You will be successful in your life. If your roots are planted in God's word every day, and you fill yourself with the promises of His scripture, you will thrive just like a tree that is planted by the water. If the tree's roots grow old in the ground, it may start to die in the soil. But, the scent of the water will help it to thrive. You can have that same mindset in life. If you're immersed in God's word, you will have hope in your heart that will last forever. Even if you're down, you know where your hope lies.

Prayer for Worried:
Dear God, please help me remember that all hope
is not lost for me even if I am down. Thank you
that through you, I have everlasting hope.

CHRIST DWELLS WITHIN YOU

"…that according to the riches of his glory he may grant you to be
strengthened with power through his Spirit in your inner being, 17
so that Christ may dwell in your hearts through faith."
Ephesians 3:16-17 ESV

You are strengthened every day by the power of the Holy Spirit. You are
made strong by your faith in Jesus. You have the power of the Holy Spirit
dwelling within you, and you have the Holy Spirit's strength readily available to you at all times. Jesus wants to strengthen your faith so that you can
do many amazing things in your life. Knowing Jesus can and will change
your life for the best. You will feel more at peace even when hard circumstances arise. You will be able to think through those difficult situations
with clarity and calmness. Your reliance on God will be strengthened every
time you call on His name. You're able to activate your faith by being positive in tough times. You can also activate your faith by praising God for His
blessings, provisions, and protection every day.

Another way that you can activate your faith is by asking Him for supernatural strength whenever you feel as though you can't take another step.
He loves you so much that He allows His Spirit to dwell in you in ways
that can only be explained by Him. You will have hope where there used
to be no hope. Instead of feeling drained, you will start to feel empowered.
Instead of being discouraged, you will feel encouraged. Instead of being
afraid, you will feel courageous. Instead of being angry at something someone said, you will be able to forgive the person and let it go. Instead of
lashing out at someone in anger, you will be able to talk to them calmly and
discuss what is causing a rift between you two. Christ is dwelling in you
right now. Take the time today to activate your faith.

PRAYER FOR HELP:
Dear God, please help me to dwell on my faith in you. Help
me to activate my hope and faith eagerly every day.

God's Calling

"I pray that the eyes of your heart may be enlightened so
that you may know what is the hope of his calling…."
Ephesians 1:18 CSB

Have you ever felt like you didn't know what your calling is in this life? You're not the only one who has ever felt like that. Everyone has gone through days of feeling inadequate. You can get out of that funk and remind yourself that God still has a great plan and purpose for your life. You can remind yourself of this scripture where it tells you that people are praying for the eyes of your heart to be opened and enlightened. People in your life- your friends and family, and even people at your church, are constantly praying for your heart to be enlightened and your eyes to be opened to the goodness, mercy, and grace of God all around you. They are praying for you to figure out your calling in life.

You can even come before God at any time and ask Him what His divine purpose is for your life. He will help you know your calling, and He will help you know what steps to take to make the desires of your heart a reality. Once you figure out your purpose and what His calling is on your life, go after it with everything you have within you. Be there for someone who is in need. Change the world with God. You can make a very big difference in someone's life just by telling them about Jesus and what He has done for you. Then you can help others find their purpose in their life. You can pray for their eyes to be opened to the purpose that God has for them. Encourage them to find their God-given purpose and tell them that even though it will be tough, God will help them make a difference in life just like He has done for you.

Prayer of Relief:
Dear God, thank you for always being my hope. Thank
you for helping me figure out my calling. Help me be an
encouragement to others who're still figuring out their calling.

GOD BELIEVES IN YOU

"Love finds no joy in unrighteousness but rejoices in the truth. 7 It bears all things, believes all things, hopes all things, endures all things."
1 Corinthians 13:6-7 CSB

God's love is the root of all things. He loves you so much that He delights in you. He wants you to know that you can always count on Him for anything, no matter what. Love is the binder of all things, and nothing can ever stop God's love for you. No matter how much you think you have screwed up in your life, there is no sin that God will not forgive you for. He wants to know whatever is on your mind and wants to help you in all areas of your life. No matter what you have done wrong, God will always take you back with open arms. Instead of thinking, "I screwed up. I have to run away from God now," He wants you to start thinking, "I'm not a lost cause after all. I can go to Him in prayer about anything I've done wrong, and He will listen to me. Thanks to Him, I am never a lost cause. Thanks to Him, I've never made too many mistakes to be unworthy of His love."

Remember, love doesn't find joy in unrighteousness. Rather, it delights in the truth. So, the next time you might be tempted to tell a small lie, remember that lying is a sin in God's eyes. But if you lie and then ask for forgiveness confessing what you did wrong, and you mean that you're sorry with all your heart, God will forgive you. He wants you to not lie about anything, no matter how tempting it could be to get away with the lie. He also wants you to remember that love bears, believes, hopes and endures all things. That means that He bears your sins for you. He believes in you at all times. He has eternal hope in you, and He believes in everything that He has created you to be.

PRAYER OF GRATITUDE:
Dear Lord, thank you for believing in me. Help me to believe in everything that you've created me to be.

CONFIDENCE FROM YOUR YOUTH

"For you are my hope, Lord God, my confidence from my youth."
Psalm 71:5 CSB

How long have you had a relationship with God? Have you known Him since you were a little kid? How have you kept hope in your heart throughout your life? Do you remember when you continually had hope in your heart when you were little? You had peace and strength that could only come from God Himself. You knew that you were being taken care of by your parents and by any other older siblings that you had. You felt secure in your life. You can continue to have that same hope and confidence that you had in your youth throughout your life. God gives you that same sense of peace, security, and hope now. All you have to do is receive it. Keep your hope in Him from the time you are young, all the way through your life, and you will have a happier life.

Even when you go through hard times, you can say affirmations of faith every day. You can say things like: "I know I can do all things through Christ who strengthens me." "I am taken care of by God. I know He is with me at all times." "God will make a way when there doesn't seem to be a way." "With God, I can conquer any obstacle that comes my way." "With God, all things are possible." When you feel unsafe, you can say things like: "I know God is protecting me from any harm." "He is placing His angels around me." "I know no harm will befall me." "I am safe in God's arms."

PRAYER FOR GUIDANCE:
Dear God, thank you for coming into my heart at a young age.
Thank you for being my confidence from my youth until now.
Help me to always keep the faith no matter what happens
in my life. Help me to keep your confidence in my heart.

Look Forward to Heaven's Glory

"He will wipe away every tear from their eyes. Death will be
no more; grief, crying, and pain will be no more,
because the previous things have passed away."
Revelation 21:4 CSB

When things on this earth seem too hard to handle, think of the glorious future that awaits you in heaven one day. On earth, you will have struggles, pain, and suffering. You will doubt yourself and your abilities. You will sincerely think that there is no way that you can be used by God to prosper His kingdom. You and your friends will grow apart, and you and your family will go through tough financial and mental hardships. There will be deaths in your family and among your friends, and there will be times when you feel as though you can't go on. The list goes on and on with the struggles that you can have on earth.

But when you get to heaven, you will have amazing sights meet your eyes. There will be no more crying, pain, or suffering. You will no longer be left feeling as if you don't measure up in God's eyes. You will never experience grief again. You will be happy forever. You get to live with God and Jesus forever. The streets will be paved with gold, and beautiful jewels will line the city walls. But these things will look plain and worthless compared to the beauty of God's glory. You will be reunited with your loved ones who have passed before you. You will get to worship God forever with your family and friends who are up in heaven with you. You will see the angels with their heavenly beauty, and you will see Jesus face to face for the first time. You will stand in His presence in awe of everything that He has done for you.

Prayer for Comfort:
Dear Lord, thank you that I have the promise of heaven waiting
for me. Thank you that I can cling to that promise of seeing you in
heaven whenever things on earth seem to be too hard to handle.
Help me to look forward to what I'll experience in heaven.

Living Hope

"Blessed be the God and Father of our Lord Jesus Christ. Because of his great mercy he has given us new birth into a living hope through the resurrection of Jesus Christ from the dead."
1 Peter 1:3 CSB

With being a Christian, you have God's hope in you at all times. When you became a Christian, you automatically were reborn and given the gift of salvation through Jesus. Jesus loved you so much that He died an agonizing death for you on the cross at Calvary. He didn't want to see you die and go to hell for your sins, so God sent Jesus, His one and only Son, to die for you. He decided to take the punishment that you rightfully deserved in your place. God and Jesus loved you so much that He willingly sacrificed His life for you. He saw how much sin was in the world, and He decided to save you and everyone on earth from the eternal punishment of sin, which is hell. Because of His sacrificial death and resurrection, you have the hope of God within you every day.

No one else in your life or your friends or family circle could ever claim that kind of love for you. Sure, your family loves you with all their hearts, and so do your friends. But none of their love can even come close to the greatness of God's love for you. He loves you beyond all the depths of your understanding.

When you became a Christian, you were given the living hope that so many people search for in their lives, but only a few people find it. You know that He has a great plan and purpose for your life. Through Jesus raising from the dead, you can help others find the everlasting hope that you have in your heart.

Prayer of Relief:
Dear God, thank you for giving me everlasting hope
through Jesus dying on the cross for me. Thank you that
I am saved through you and you alone. Thank you for the
opportunity to tell others about the hope I have in you.

God Will Not Change His Mind

"God is not a man, that he might lie, or a son of man, that he might change his mind. Does he speak and not act, or promise and not fulfill?"
Numbers 23:19 CSB

Remember what it says in this scripture whenever you are left wondering if and when God might fulfill His promises to you. God isn't a man. Men on earth lie. But God is not from earth. He's from heaven, and He would never let you down or lie to you to protect your feelings. Rather He wants to tell you the promises in His word are true. God is also not a son of man. A son of man is an earthly person who can and will change his mind at a moment's notice if the position or situation doesn't seem to fit their lifestyle. Once God makes up His mind to deliver you or to help change your life around, He will move in mighty ways to make good things happen for you in your life. He will never take a look at your life and say, "well, maybe I'll help this person. Oh, wait, maybe I won't." He will never change His mind. There is nothing God won't do for you in your life. Call on His name, and He will answer you.

God is holy, just, fair, and He is loving. He loves you beyond description and more than you could fathom. This scripture even asks you if God speaks and then doesn't act for you upon your behalf. The exact opposite of that is true. Whenever God acts upon the good of your behalf in this earthly life, you will see the most unexpected and great things happen for you. Sometimes, you won't even be able to describe how good you feel knowing that God is moving things around on your behalf.

Prayer for Guidance:
Dear Lord, please help me to remember that you will always come through on your words. Thank you for your promises are always true and that I can always count on you no matter what.

HEALTH AND HEALING

*"But I will bring you health and will heal you of your wounds—
this is the Lord's declaration—for they call you Outcast,
Zion whom no one cares about."*
Jeremiah 30:17 CSB

Whenever your health is declining or failing, you might start doubting that God is there for you. You might start thinking that maybe God doesn't love you, or at the very least, that He doesn't care about you. But that couldn't be further from the truth. Even though your health and spirit may be declining, it doesn't mean that God doesn't care about you or that He isn't there for you. He has not abandoned you. He will never abandon you or leave you hung out to dry. When your health starts to decline, He wants you to call upon His name for healing and joy. He wants to restore the joy you once had in your life, and He wants you to know that He is there for you no matter what you're going through. He wants you to tell Him exactly how you're feeling. Don't be afraid to admit your fears to Him.

Tell Him that you are scared of losing your health or even scared of dying. Tell Him that you are afraid of losing all hope or even that you've already started to lose all hope. Tell Him that you aren't sure how things will play out and that you need His reassurance to calm your anxious heart. Tell Him that you want to believe in His everlasting promises again. He will bring you healing from your sickness and your pain. He will heal you from your wounds. All you have to do is call on Him and believe that you will be healed. He will deliver you from all your hurt. You may not be healed in your lifetime on earth, but you will be healed fully once you reach heaven.

PRAYER FOR WORRIED:
Dear God, please heal me from my wounds. Please bring
healing to my body, soul, and mind through your power. Thank
you that I can call on you for eternal healing at any time.

Have a Joyful Heart

"A joyful heart is good medicine, but a broken spirit dries up the bones."
Proverbs 17:22 CSB

Having a joyful heart can be difficult when you are going through something that seems impossible to get through. When you are struggling to keep faith in your heart, you often start believing that things won't possibly get any better. You may have stomach pain, anxiety or panic attacks, and other problems. But having a joyful heart can bring you so many benefits. You will feel more peace in your heart. You will have more clarity in your mind, and you will be able to find joy even in the most unpleasant circumstances. You won't have as many anxieties or panic attacks. You will be able to see things with joy.

Being able to be joyful even in hard times will make people wonder why you feel that way. They might even ask you why you are so optimistic about your life and why you are more at peace than the average person. It will allow you to be a witness to them and to tell them about Jesus. If you're unsure about what to say, here are a few tips: "Even though things are hard right now, I know that God will deliver me from this problem." "I have the peace of God in my heart. I have the hope that surpasses all understanding in my heart." "You can have the peace of God in your life and have the same joy I have. If you want to, let's pray together right now, and you can ask Jesus into your heart." "God has worked miracles in my life, and He can work them in your life too. All you have to do is believe in Him with all your heart. He wants you to have peace and joy in your life too." You can learn to enjoy things and be joyful no matter what happens. Choose to start being joyful today.

Prayer for Comfort:
Dear God, please help me to remember that all
hope is not lost. Help me to remember that having
joy is much better than having a bitter heart.

PATIENCE OF HOPE

*"…remembering without ceasing your work of faith,
labor of love, and patience of hope in our Lord Jesus
Christ in the sight of our God and Father…."*
1 Thessalonians 1:3 NKJV

Working on keeping the faith can be difficult throughout your life. You probably have wondered time and time again, "why does it take so much work to keep my faith strong?" God knew it takes a lot of work to keep your faith strong throughout your life, but He lets storms come into your life to strengthen your reliance on Him. He doesn't want you to give up in times of trouble. Rather, He wants you to keep the patience of hope in your heart at all times. He knows that you will fail at times, but He knows how He will bring you through those hard times.

The labor of love that you have for your friends and family, and even for God Himself, can wear you out at certain times. It gets tiring taking care of everyone else's needs all the time. You can get exhausted taking care of your family's needs when they are sick or taking care of your friends whenever they are going through a bad breakup. You will lose your patience with your kids at more than one time throughout your life. But through all of those times, God knows that you are trying your best in everything you're doing. He will help you stay strong in your labor of love for your kids, your marriage, and your friends. He will help you stay strong in your faith when you feel like giving up. He will help you stay strong in the work of your faith by allowing you to come to Him about things that are happening in life. He wants you to come to Him for everything. He wants you to have the patience of hope so you can keep calm in every situation.

PRAYER FOR GUIDANCE:
Dear Lord, please help me stay strong in my hope and patience
no matter who I'm interacting with. Help me show your love to
everyone around me and be your example in everything I do.

HOPE IS NOT CUT OFF

"So shall the knowledge of wisdom be to your soul; If you have found it, there is a prospect, and your hope will not be cut off."
Proverbs 24:14 NJKV

The knowledge of wisdom comes from God. All you have to do is ask Him for it, and He will give it to you. The knowledge of wisdom will help you better understand how to deal with things in your life. You will have peace through difficult times, and you will be able to say with confidence, "God will deliver me from my enemies. God will make a way when there seems to be no way." When things are difficult, you will be able to carry the hope of God throughout your life, and through that hope, you will be able to bless others around you. You will be able to tell them, "God will never abandon you. God will give you the wisdom that you need to face the problem you're dealing with. He will give you the ability to rise again out of the very thing you thought would bury you."

Through speaking wisdom to your friends and family about God, you will be able to help them overcome what might seem impossible to them. You will be able to help them remain strong in their faith. You can remind them that God is never far away from them and that they can call on Him at any time.

If you have found wisdom, God has a plan and purpose for your life, and no matter how dark things seem, your hope is not cut off forever. Remember, it is almost always darkest right before dawn. That means that right before your breakthrough, you will think it's time to give up. However, that is when God whispers, "my child, I have you." Right when you feel like giving up, that's when God allows some great things to happen in your life to remind you of His glory.

PRAYER FOR COMFORT:
Dear Lord, thank you for giving me the hope that will never be cut off. Thank you for giving me your knowledge. Please help me to rely on you for the knowledge I need.

Do Not Pity Yourself

"If in this life only we have hope in Christ,
we are of all men the most pitiable."
1 Corinthians 15:19 NKJV

Having hope in Christ is the most important thing in your life. You can enjoy things that much easier. Having hope in Christ means you have the glory of God to look forward to when you get to heaven. Even if you only have God's hope in you throughout your life, it is still better than having no hope at all. You are given the gift of glory. Even though it says in the scripture that you are to be pitied because you have the hope of God within you, you don't have to look at yourself with pity. Instead, be proud that you have the hope of God flowing in your body, soul, and mind. Enjoy the fact that you have a calm mind and peace within your body. You are blessed to have hope for the future. You're blessed to have a relationship with God.

But others will see your relationship with God as something to be pitied. They don't understand the value of a relationship with Him. They might say, "Boy, this person is strange to have hope in something that they can't see. How can they have hope in something or someone they can't see? If God is so good in their lives and is so good to them, how come bad things keep happening? Let's pity them instead of rejoicing with them that they have a relationship with God." The people may even mock you for having hope that they don't understand. That allows you to witness to them and to tell them about God. Even though people may pity you because of your relationship with God, you can explain that He is the one who gives you hope to carry on when no one else can. He also gives you the strength to carry on amid life's trials in a way that no one else can.

Prayer for Help:
Dear God, thank you for allowing me to have hope in my
life. Thank you for helping me be a witness for you.

GOD HEARS YOU

"For in You, O Lord, I hope; You will hear, O Lord my God."
Psalm 38:15 NKJV

How amazing is it to know that the God of the universe hears you? He hears you when you pray for hope in the stillness of your heart, out loud, with a group of friends, or inside a church, or out in nature. No matter where you are, you can come to Him. Even if you're in a car on the high-way, stuck in the middle of a traffic jam, you can come to Him in prayer. He always wants to hear from you. He wants to fill you with hope and peace that surpasses all human understanding. He wants you to know that no matter how big or small your prayers may be, He hears you.

So, the next time you are tempted to give up, turn your worries over to God. Ask Him for the things you need, and He will help you. He will restore the hope that once was lost to you. He will give you the peace that you didn't know you were missing. When you come to Him in prayer, you can tell Him exactly what is on your mind without fear of judgment. He loves you so much, and He sees you as His precious child. He already knows exactly what is on your mind before you even speak a word. Tell Him how you're feeling and ask Him to help you. Let Him know how close you are to los-ing hope again and ask Him to restore it for you. Whenever you come to Him in prayer, you don't have to worry about how goofy your prayers may sound. Thank Him for the ability to pour your heart out before Him at any time, anywhere. Thank Him for His outpouring of love and for giving your hope back when you needed it the most.

PRAYER OF GRATITUDE:

Dear Lord, thank you for the privilege to come before you in prayer. Thank you for always hearing my prayers. Thank you for filling my life with the hope of the life to come.

STEADFAST IN THE LORD

"He will not be afraid of evil tidings;
His heart is steadfast, trusting in the Lord."
Psalm 112:7 NKJV

You do not need to fear when you have faith in God. At times, it can be hard not to let the sinking feelings of 'what if' scenarios plague your mind, especially if you're struggling severely. It can feel as if God is distant from you or that He has abandoned you completely when you aren't getting the answer to your prayers as fast as you would like.

This scripture says that you don't have to fear anything evil in your life. That means that you don't have to be afraid of Satan's schemes or anyone else's schemes throughout your life. Even though there are times to fear in your life, God doesn't want you to constantly live in fear. He wants you to keep His everlasting hope in your heart. He wants you to remember that you are His and that nothing will ever snatch you out of His hands. Remembering that God is with you every step of the way can be difficult at times, but you can remind yourself of His promises. You can turn any worrisome thought into words of affirmation by telling yourself that God has never left you and that He never will. You can turn your worries into worship and sing them away. You can say: "God helped my family through the last difficult time; he will do it again." "I will overcome my mental and emotional struggles with God's help." "God is watching over my family." Whenever Satan tries to make you second guess God, remind him of his future. God already defeated him by dying on the cross for your sins and rising from the grave. Try your best not to give in to negative thoughts. Instead, fill your heart with hope. Keep your heart steadfast in the promises of the Lord, and you will feel more peace and security as you walk through your day-to-day life.

PRAYER OF COMFORT:
Dear God, please help me to focus on you instead of
negative thoughts. Help me to trust you more and more
each day. Thank you that you're always with me.

LIFTED UP

"For the day of the Lord of hosts shall come upon everything proud and lofty, upon everything lifted up—And it shall be brought low—"
Isaiah 2:12 NKJV

When God comes to take everyone to heaven with Him, He will come upon everything proudly and joyfully. All believers will be lifted to eternity in heaven. Everyone proud shall be brought low, so they too can see the goodness of God. Everyone who doesn't know Him will be brought low and cast into hell. But God wants everyone to know Him and have a personal relationship with Him. He promises He will never leave you or forsake you. He will always help you through your problems, and He will give you strength, perseverance, and endurance to keep going even when you want to quit. He will cover you with His wings of refuge whenever you need shelter from the storms of life or the storms in your mind. He will always fight for you no matter what you're going through and no matter what you have done.

One day you will be brought up to heaven and raised to glory to be with Jesus forever. Let that thought keep you going whenever you want to give up hope. You will get to experience heaven forever with the people who have gone before you. Everything on earth will be brought to a lower state when God comes again. Keep your eyes on the prize of heaven every single day. Try your best not to be too proud of yourself. Instead, stay humble, especially when things are going well for you. Remember that God is the source of your success in life and that you couldn't accomplish anything on your own or in your power. Remember to thank God every day for the blessings that you have in your life.

PRAYER FOR GUIDANCE:
Dear God, please help me not to ever be too proud about the way my life is. Help me to stay humble and kind throughout my life. Thank you that I will get to be in heaven with you one day.

MOVE MOUNTAINS WITH FAITH

"So Jesus said to them, "Because of your unbelief; for assuredly,
I say to you, if you have faith as a mustard seed, you will say to
this mountain, 'Move from here to there,' and it will move;
and nothing will be impossible for you."
Mathew 17:20 NJKV

One of the most awesome promises that you can cling to when your hope is wearing thin is: if you have even just a little bit of faith in yourself, you will be able to do great things. If you believe that you will be able to walk through storms in your life, God will give you the strength to do it. If you believe in supernatural healing for yourself or a friend, He will grant it if it's His will. He may not give you or your friend healing on this side of heaven, but whenever the time comes to be in heaven, the healing will be fulfilled.

If you have faith as small as a mustard seed that you will be able to deliver a great presentation at work, God will help you do just that. Thinking positive thoughts doesn't mean that you think that you're better than anyone else. It also doesn't mean that you won't have struggles in your life. It just means that whenever a struggle comes, that you have peace and hope from God in your heart. You know that through faith in Jesus, nothing will be impossible for you.

Yes, things will be difficult, but you will be able to get through them with a lot more peace and clarity with God than if you didn't have faith in God. Sometimes having faith as small as a mustard seed is all it takes for miraculous things to happen. Never be afraid to say "move" to any mountain in your life because it will move in God's timing and His ways.

PRAYER OF RELIEF:
Dear God, please help me to keep my faith in you, no matter
how little faith I might have. Help take what little faith I
have and make it as strong as you possibly can. Thank you
for helping me move many mountains with my faith.

Suffering for Christ

"For to this end we both labor and suffer reproach, because we trust in the living God, who is the Savior of all men, especially of those who believe."
1 Timothy 4:10 NKJV

In your life, you will labor through difficulty and suffer because you believe in God. You will go through valleys of the shadow of death and think that there is no way out, but God will carry you through. He is the Savior of all things and the Savior of all men. Even though He will let your faith be tested to the very brink, He will not let you be tested beyond what you can bear. If you believe in God, you have the eternal hope of heaven in your heart at all times. You know that even though you will go through difficulty, this world is not your home. You know you have a place in heaven with God waiting for you.

The world will come at you with constant hate and criticism because you believe in God. Even though you will be attacked on all sides, God has you under His wings. Rest under His refuge and be content with your decision to follow Jesus. You know it will continue to change and help your life in marvelous ways that only you and God can understand. So, the next time you go through the suffering of any kind, remember that it's ok to have suffering as a Christian. Having suffering will only strengthen your reliance on God. It will help you get closer to Him when you need Him the most. Getting closer to God will help you be able to withstand more trials than you ever expected. It will make you a stronger person. When you face criticism for your faith, you can boldly tell the people criticizing you that you're not going to be deterred by their mean and hateful comments.

PRAYER OF GUIDANCE:
Dear Lord, please help me not to give in to the constant criticism about my faith. Help me to stand strong when I'm being ridiculed for my faith. Help any criticism of my faith strengthen my reliance on you.

GLORY REVEALED IN HEAVEN

"For I consider that the sufferings of this present time are not worthy to be compared with the glory which shall be revealed in us."
Romans 8:18 NKJV

There will be struggles and trials that you go through in your life. But there will never be a struggle that you go through without God being in your corner. You may think that you're at the end of your rope, and that is when God carries you through to the other side. No matter how bad things seem, there is nothing God won't get you through. Take a look back on your life. What are some things that you thought you wouldn't be able to get through? Maybe it was the death of a close family member or friend or getting diagnosed with an illness with no cure. Maybe you got fired from your job. Even though it seemed as if there was no way out of those situations, God got you through.

Now think about your life in the present. Maybe your child is struggling in school or college. Maybe you're struggling financially, or you're struggling emotionally. No matter what you are facing, your present sufferings in this world are nothing compared to the glorious riches that await you in heaven. So instead of dwelling on how bad things are right now, remember that you have already won the victory through Christ. You are bought with His blood, and no matter how bad the battle is right now, you have already won the war. Jesus paid the ultimate price by dying on the cross for you. Keep this thought in your mind whenever you face trials- "this battle is difficult, but I will one day be in heaven forever." Nothing on this earth, no pain or suffering that you go through, have gone through, or any suffering that you have yet to go through, will ever compare to the glories of heaven.

PRAYER OF COMFORT:
Dear Lord, please help me to remember the hope of your promise. Thank you for the promise that the pain I have now can't compare to the glory that awaits me in heaven.

MERCIES ARE NEW EVERY MORNING

"This I recall to my mind; Therefore, I have hope. Through the Lord's mercies we are not consumed. Because His compassions fail not. They are new every morning; Great is Your faithfulness."
Lamentations 3:21-23 NKJV

Hope is one of the most beautiful emotions you can ever feel. It fills you with optimism when the rest of the world says you should be filled with dread. It makes you feel happier about the future instead of being afraid of it. It tells you that God has a plan and purpose for your life when the world and Satan whisper, "you screwed up too much. There is nothing left to hope for." When life gets difficult, do you cling to the hope that things will get better instead of thinking about how things can worsen? Even though there are and will be difficult days in your life, you will not be consumed or overpowered by them because of God's mercy and grace. When things get difficult, you can turn to God and ask Him to help you turn things around. You can ask Him to keep the hope in your heart overflowing.

Allow your heart to overflow with joy, knowing that God's compassion will never fail you. Because of the Lord's mercies, you are not consumed by the trials of this world. Rather, each trial has made you stronger, and each trial that you go through will continue to make you stronger. Each new day you can wake up telling God, "Thank you for another day of life." You can thank Him that His mercies abound in your life. Every day is a blessing. Take the time to look at the blessings of your life. You are alive and breathing. You're able to work and provide for your family. You have a house or apartment, and you have family and friends that love you. Thank Him for being there for you and for reminding you of His faithfulness.

PRAYER OF GRATITUDE:
Dear God, please help me to focus on the blessings in my life each day. Thank you for your never-ending love, mercy and grace. Thank you for showing your faithfulness to me every day.

There is Hope

"You are wearied in the length of your way; Yet you did not say,
'There is no hope.' You have found the life of your hand;
Therefore, you were not grieved."
Isaiah 57:10 NJKV

Even though everyday life can get you down, you don't have to give in to the negative thoughts that Satan tries to put in your mind. He tries to make you think that you won't be able to do certain things, that you are not capable of greatness, and that things are just too much for you to handle.

Even though you will get tired along the way, with God on your side, the journey of your life will be a lot easier. Even though you are exhausted, you don't ever have to start believing that there is no hope. There is always something to hope for because you have a relationship with God. There is always something to hope in. The goodness of God is all around you every day. All you have to do is search them out and start recognizing them.

You can always have hope in God, no matter what is happening in your life. No matter what life throws at you, don't give in to the negative thought that there is no hope. As long as you have God in your life, there is always hope available to you at a moment's notice. All you have to do is ask Him to change your attitude from negative to positive, and He will move in mighty ways to reveal His power in your life. Jesus is the reason that you have hope in the midst of dark times, and He is the reason why you're able to persevere during those times. Instead of crumbling to the floor in defeat, you can rise above your circumstances and say, "I know God has me. I'm not going to be pushed down by my circumstances. I'm not going to wallow in sadness. Instead, I choose hope and joy."

Prayer for Help:
Dear God, please help me to rise above every
circumstance with hope in my heart. Help me to
call on you whenever I feel like giving up.

GOD IS YOUR REFUGE

I will say of the Lord, "He is my refuge and my fortress;
My God, in Him I will trust."
Psalm 91:2 NKJV

Who do you turn to for guidance, strength, and endurance in your life? Do you turn to the world for those things, or do you turn to Jesus for them? When life knocks you down, how often do you stay in that place? Do you pray and get back on your feet as soon as possible? Or do you wallow in pity, asking why certain things happen to you? Instead of having a pity party, you can tell yourself that this hard place that you're in right now is not permanent. You don't have to stay miserable forever. You can choose joy and peace throughout your life. You can say things like: "I know He will provide for me. God is my refuge and my strength." "I turn to Him, and I know He hears me." "Even though it feels like He is silent at times, I know He is never far away. I know He is working behind the scenes of my life." "God is my rock, my refuge, and my fortress." "I know that He will provide a way even when there seems to be no way."

Once you start talking positively, your life will start going more positively. You can start thinking positively. Whenever a negative thought creeps into your head, remember how blessed you are instead of dwelling on how stressed you are. Hope can change your life. All it takes is one positive thought to turn your day around. Once you make hope your daily habit, it will become your weekly habit, and soon you will be so used to thinking positively about your life that you will not be as bothered by negative thoughts or feelings. Remember, the Lord is with you. He wants to be your refuge and strength throughout your life. Allow Him to be present in your life.

PRAYER FOR COMFORT:
Dear God, please help me to have hope and trust in
you. Help me not to have a pity party whenever life gets
difficult, but to look at the blessings of my life.

Run the Race with Hope

"Being confident of this very thing, that He who has begun a good
ork in you will complete it until the day of Jesus Christ;"
Philippians 1:6 NJKV

God will not let you down. When it feels as though things couldn't be worse, that is when Satan gets under your skin and in your mind, trying to keep you from remembering that you are God's child. He will try and make you second guess yourself and your abilities. But God continually whispers to your heart, "keep trying. I am with you. You don't have to give up all hope. Don't give in to Satan's lies. Listen to my words of truth, prosperity, peace, and hope."

You can have hope in your heart every day because God began a good work in you before you were even born. He brought your dreams and goals to life in your heart at a young age. He will help you know that He is taking everything that Satan meant for your harm, and He will use it for your good. He will help you complete each task that He has set out for you with calmness, peace, and clarity. He began a good work in you, and He will help you do amazing things every day of your life until the day God calls you home to be with Him. God will help you do the things He has called you to do with hope in your heart. Hope for today and tomorrow, as well as the years to come. You have an amazing life ahead of you. Embrace it knowing that God has a beautiful plan for you. Have confidence that whatever He started in your life, He will help you finish it. Whatever dreams you have inside you, let God take the wheel of your life and bring those dreams to pass. Run the race of your life with hope in your heart.

Prayer of Gratitude:
Dear God, please help me to be confident in the promises
you made me. Thank you that you put dreams into my
heart and set a great life before me. Thank you for helping
me run the race of life with hope in my heart.

WAITING FOR GOD

"And now, Lord, what do I wait for? My hope is in You."
Psalm 39:7 NKJV

When you're waiting for things to get better, you're often missing out on the blessings that God has given you in the present. You could be missing out on the blessings all around you by not focusing on the good things in your life. You have probably experienced waiting for people to change their behavior, whether it was your kids, spouse, boss, family members, parents, or friends. Waiting for everyone else to change will only make your life harder. You have to be the one who is willing to make changes in your life, no matter how hard things get. Even if no one else is willing to make the changes they need to make in their life, be willing to make the changes you need to make to have a better life.

While you're waiting for things to get better, do you put your hope in God, or do you hope in the world? If you put your hope in the world, then you will be let down and disappointed very quickly. People will let you down and disappoint you. But God will never disappoint you. If you put your hope in Him, He will help you through all difficulties that you face. When you put your hope in Him, you will see amazing things start to happen in your life. You will have more clarity and peace of mind whenever struggles arise, and you will be able to talk yourself out of thinking negatively.

You will be able to say that you know that God is in control of your life. You will have peace, and you will know that God is taking care of every situation that you find yourself in. When you can keep your hope in Him, you will have calmness in your heart no matter the circumstances.

PRAYER FOR GUIDANCE:
Dear Lord, please help me put my hope in you and not wait
to make my life better. Help me make it better today.

Be Still

"You will not need to fight in this battle. Position yourselves, stand still and see the salvation of the Lord, who is with you, O Judah and Jerusalem!"
2 Chronicles 20:17 NKJV

How amazing is it to know that God is already fighting your battles for you before they even begin? Before anything even started to bother you, God already had the solution to each and every one of your problems and obstacles. He knows exactly how each one will affect you. God wants you to not always stress over fighting battles in your life. Instead, He wants you to come to Him when facing any battles. He also wants you to remember that sometimes the best thing you can do is be still and trust in Him, even when you want to act impulsively to solve your problems. Solving your problems under your power can only cause you more stress. Plus, it can make you think that you don't need to rely on Him for the strength you need to get through life's battles.

Sometimes being still and letting God have complete control over the situation that you find yourself in is the absolute best thing you can do. It gives you the chance to surrender any plans you had in that moment and place them all in God's hands where they rightfully belong. As it says in this scripture, position yourself to see the salvation of the Lord. Stand still and bask in the hope that no matter what battles you face in your life, God is fighting for you in ways that only He can. If He can continually fight for Jerusalem and Judah, He will surely fight for you in your life. There is no battle that He is not deep in the trenches with you. Trust in Him and cling to the hope that He can and will carry you through any battles you face. He is, has been, and always will be fighting your battles for you.

Prayer for Guidance:
Dear God, whenever I face battles in my life, please help me to remember to be still. Help me to trust that you're fighting for me.

HOPE FOR THE FUTURE

"For I know the thoughts that I think toward you, says the Lord, thoughts of peace and not of evil, to give you a future and a hope."
Jeremiah 29:11 NJKV

God knows what He truly thinks of you. You are His beloved child, and He only wants the best for you. At times you will make mistakes, and you will feel as though you're not worthy of being in His presence. But He encourages you to come to Him, whether you feel worthy to talk to Him or not. He loves you more than your mom, dad, husband or wife, or friends can ever love you. He loved you so much that He died on the cross willingly, taking your punishment as His own. No one else in your life has ever done that for you.

Yes, your friends and family would most likely die for you without even thinking twice about it, but Jesus already died for you to secure your place in heaven. He wants to give you peace and not have anything evil harm you. He wants to fill you with hope for your future and for you to get excited about the things that are to come in your life. He wants you to remember that the best things in life are yet to come. God wants you to keep His everlasting hope in your heart at all times. He wants you to be happy and enjoy every moment of your life. He has amazing plans for you. Ask Him to guide you in everything you do, and He will direct your path. He never wants you to forget the hope of His promises.

He has never thought anything evil towards you, from the second you were born until now. God only wants to give you the best, most fulfilling life possible. He wants you to have hope for every day that is ahead of you. He wants you to have peace as you go through tough circumstances.

PRAYER FOR WORRIED:
Dear Lord, please help me to trust in your plan for my
life. Help me to look to you for hope in my life.

WAITING ON GOD

"But those who wait on the Lord shall renew their strength;
They shall mount up with wings like eagles. They shall run
and not be weary. They shall walk and not faint."
Isaiah 40:31 NJKV

Waiting for the Lord is not easy. It can be one of the hardest things to do. It can seem as if God is always testing your faith to see if you're relying on Him for everything instead of relying on Him once in a while.

This scripture says those who wait on the Lord will renew their strength. They will soar through life like eagles soaring on the wind. Those who trust in God will run and not grow weary, and they will walk and not be faint. That means that no matter the difficulties you face in your life, as long as you have faith, hope, and trust in God, you will prevail. Trusting in God is something you will learn how to do throughout your life. But the sooner you learn to wait on God; the easier your life will become. You will feel stronger and more able to complete hard tasks.

The sooner you learn to trust in Him and thank Him for the blessings you have in good times, the easier it will be to trust Him and to thank Him in hard times. Wouldn't you like to have wings to soar like an eagle? Wouldn't you like to run and not grow weary and walk and not faint? That's the power of God at work in your life. Once you learn to rely on His power, you will be able to get through circumstances much easier. Whenever you are tempted to do things under your power, take a step back and remember you can always turn to God. Remember that God wants you to wait on Him to renew your strength.

PRAYER OF COMFORT:
Dear Lord, please help me wait on you when all I want
is to figure out life in my own power. Help me trust in
you when I start thinking that I can figure things out
on my own. Thank you for helping me trust in you.

HEIRS TO HEAVEN

"that having been justified by His grace we should become
heirs according to the hope of eternal life."
Titus 3:7 NKJV

You have the hope of eternal life inside you as soon as you trust in God. Through faith, you are justified to God by His power, mercy, love, and grace. You are an heir to the hope of eternal life through salvation in Jesus. How amazing is it to know that you are accepted by God Himself as a holy and precious heir to the glorious riches of heaven? You are given the most precious gift of salvation. You get to have a personal relationship with Jesus as your Lord and Savior.

You have every opportunity to tell others about the hope you have received through salvation in Christ. Let them know that they too can become right with God and become heirs to the hope of heaven. All they have to do is confess that they want to have Jesus transform their lives and come into their hearts, and their lives will be forever changed. By His grace, they will be brought to heaven one day when He calls every believer home. He wants everyone to know of His goodness, mercy, and grace in their lives, and He wants you to know that no matter what you have done, you are saved through Him alone.

You have the hope of eternal life within you at all times. Embrace that hope and let it excite you. You are an heir to the eternity of heaven. Whenever He calls you home, you get to live forever with Jesus and the rest of your family members who have gone before you. In heaven, there will be no more pain, sorrow, gnashing of teeth, criticism, or any other type of physical, mental, or emotional pain. No matter what happens in your life, you can look forward to going to heaven with hope.

PRAYER FOR GUIDANCE:
Dear God, thank you that I am justified by my faith. Thank you that I am an heir to heaven. Thank you that you are preparing a place for me. Thank you for my salvation.

A New Creation

"Therefore, if anyone is in Christ, he is a new creation; old things
have passed away; behold, all things have become new."
2 Corinthians 5:17

If you believe in Christ, you are a brand-new creation. The old version of
yourself is now gone, and you are a completely new and different person.
Embrace being a new creation through your faith in God and allow His
peace to come over you in ways you never experienced before. Allow yourself to be immersed in your new faith. Explore the Bible every chance you
get and enjoy your fellowship time with other believers. Come before God
and ask Him to reveal new and exciting things about Himself to you. If you
have questions about God, ask them to a family member, friend, or pastor.
There is nothing wrong with asking questions and getting them answered.
It is an amazing feeling to know that God has taken the old, messed up
version of you and replaced it with a brand-new one.

He doesn't see you as messed up, inadequate, or not worthy. Rather, He sees
you as a person He literally can't live without. You were bought with a precious price, and He wants you to have His hope in Him throughout your
life. No matter what you have done in your past, if you ask for forgiveness
and mean it with all of your heart, He will make it as if you never even
sinned. He will wipe every sin and every wrongdoing that you have ever
committed off of your record. He will make you spotless. He loves you that
much! Every day is a chance for you to embrace Him and proclaim how He
has changed your life, renewed you, and made you a better person. Embrace
the fact that you are a brand-new person through Jesus and His ultimate
sacrifice for you.

Prayer of Relief:
Dear God, please help me remember that I am a new
creation through my faith in you. Thank you that the old
version of me has passed away and that every day you are
renewing me, strengthening me, and making me whole.

You Will Rise Again

"Do not rejoice over me, my enemy; When I fall, I will arise;
When I sit in darkness, The Lord will be a light to me."
Micah 7:8 NKJV

Sometimes it feels as though this world is against you. You feel pressed from all sides, and you don't know what to do. The weight of the world feels like it's coming down on your shoulders in all areas of your life. People may like to see you be worn out physically, mentally, emotionally, and even spiritually. But those days of feeling worn out won't last forever. When God sees another person rejoicing over you when you are in pain, He will do everything in His power to help you rise even stronger than before. You can even tell the person who may be rejoicing over your struggles that you know God will vindicate you. You know God will help you.

Even though you have fallen, with God's help, you won't stay down for very long. You can tell people that you have hope in your heart from an everlasting source, and that's Jesus. He's the one who gives you strength when you feel as though you can't continue. He is the one who picks you up and carries you to the finish line right in front of your enemies who thought you were down for the count. He will light a way for you and help you understand what He is capable of doing in your life. Whenever you stumble and fall, remind yourself that God is already moving in ways that no one can stop. You don't have to lose hope while being surrounded by your enemies. When they see you down, remind them not to be harsh or say that you won't get back up. Remind them that through God, you will rise again. You will beat whatever obstacle you're up against. You have the power of God in you, and you will be victorious.

Prayer of Comfort:
Dear Lord, please help me remember that I am
victorious in all areas of my life through you. Thank you
that you are lifting me in front of my enemies.

TAKE GOD'S HAND

"When you pass through the waters, I will be with you; And through the rivers, they shall not overflow you. When you walk through the fire, you shall not be burned, Nor shall the flame scorch you."
Isaiah 43:1-2 NKJV

God will never let you go through something without giving you a way out of it. When you feel as though you are drowning under all the pressures of life, call on Him. He promises to be with you. When you pass through rough waters, He will be with you, and the waves of frustration, despair, and uncertainty will not overcome you. All you have to do is call on Him to deliver you from your strife. He will fill you with His hope and peace. Even though it can feel as though you're drowning in the storms of life, He is always there saying to you, "my child. I'm right here. Reach for my hand, and I will pull you up out of the waters of life that are trying to consume you. Instead of looking towards the world for help, look to me. I'll get you out of whatever situation you are in. I will get you through."

When you walk through the fires of life, through God's mercy, you will not be burned. He will keep you safe. Let that thought fill you with the hope that God will never let you down.

When you feel the fires of life surrounding you, God says to you, "my child, as long as you are mine, the flames will not touch you. Instead of being overwhelmed by this life, look to me, and I will give you a place to catch your breath and recharge. Reach out. Take my hand. I will pull you through the fires without letting them destroy you. You will be victorious over the battles you face." Remember to talk to Him and to trust Him the next time life threatens to take you down.

PRAYER FOR HELP:
Dear God, please help me to take your hand and not let go during rough times. Thank you that you are leading me through those times. Please help me trust you more and more.

Be Content

*"Let your conduct be without covetousness; be content with
such things as you have. For He Himself has said, "I will never
leave you nor forsake you." So, we may boldly say: "The Lord
is my helper; I will not fear. What can man do to me?"*
Hebrews 13:5-6 NKJV

When you feel as though you are starting to covet something that someone else has, Satan has made you ungrateful for the things God has already blessed you with. Sure, you'll go through times where you feel like you should have nicer things. But God wants you to be content with the things you have in your life. He doesn't want you to be envious of other people's possessions. He wants you to take a look around and be thankful for the things you do have. He wants you to remember to be hopeful in difficult times and loving towards everyone you meet. Even though it can be difficult, He knows that you can do it.

The Lord is your helper, and He tells you not to fear anybody or anything in your life. He wants you to have the hope and confidence that He will take care of you. He will sustain you and provide for you in ways that you can't even imagine. You can have the hope that God will provide for you in many different ways. You can confess the hope that you are taken care of by God. No matter what may come your way, you can rely on God to get you through. You can confess the hope that God loves you and that no matter what may happen to you, you know the people and things of this world do not have to get you down. You can boldly say, "I know God's in control. What can man do to me? I will not covet anything anybody else has. I am grateful for what I have, especially for the hope that I have in Jesus."

Prayer of Relief:
Dear God, please help me to not covet anything anyone
else has. Instead, let me confess the hope I have in you.

Born of God

*"For whatever is born of God overcomes the world. And this
is the victory that has overcome the world—our faith."*
1 John 5:4 NKJV

When you accepted Christ as your Savior and let Him into your life, you changed your life for the better. Whoever is born of God overcomes the world. He died to save you from your sin and self-destructive ways. Your victory is through your faith in God alone. Think about it for a second; you have overcome the world by just knowing Jesus Christ as your Lord and Savior. No matter what happens, you have already received the ultimate victory through your faith. That means that you don't have to worry about the struggles of life because you know that you have the victory in Christ. God will help you rise again, this time with His power. You can overcome the world just by being who you are in Jesus. When you are born of God, you are automatically an overcomer.

Shout His name from the rooftops every chance you get. Proclaim that you are a child of God boldly every chance you get. Be a friend to someone in need. Help those who need help. Visit those who are sick. Invite people to your church to experience the hope and glory of the Gospel. Be there for your friends and family members who are going through hard times. Enjoy your life to the fullest. Claim the victory that you have through your faith in Jesus. Let people around you know that they too can have the same victory through knowing Christ as their Lord and Savior. You will get through anything in your life as long as you keep your faith. He gives you the strength, perseverance, and willpower to keep going through any trial. Your faith will see you through anything. Use your faith and rely on God every day. You are victorious through your faith. Claim it, proclaim it, and enjoy your victory every day!

PRAYER OF COMFORT:
Dear Lord, thank you that I am victorious in my
faith through my relationship with you. Help me to
receive it, proclaim it, and enjoy the victory.

No Weapon Formed Against You

"No weapon formed against you shall prosper, and every tongue which rises against you in judgment you shall condemn. This is the heritage of the servants of the Lord, and their righteousness is from Me," says the Lord."
Isaiah 54:17 NKJV

Isn't it comforting to know that God will not let any weapon formed against you prosper? How amazing is it that He thinks that highly of you to protect you like that? He loves you so much that He protects you every day from harm. Sometimes, you will not even know that there were people or things out there in the middle of your life that were ready to do you harm. God stopped them from harming you before they even got a chance to act. Every person that rises against you and tries to speak evil of you, He condemns them and protects you from them.

Whenever someone tries to speak badly about you, you can counteract their meanness by telling them that you forgive them, that God loves them, and that there is still hope left for them. You can invite them to let Jesus into their hearts in the same way you did. Whenever someone rises against you, you can cling to the hope that God gives you that their weapons of words and actions towards you will not prosper. You are a servant of the Lord, and you have your heritage from Him. He loves it when you speak about the hope you have from Him in front of your enemies. He will always protect you from harm, and He makes you righteous in His eyes. Take great comfort in the fact that He is constantly looking out for you and wants the best for you. He wants your physical, mental, emotional, and spiritual well-being to be fully protected. You get your righteousness and the ultimate source of protection from God Himself. Claim it, and enjoy it in every way that you can.

PRAYER OF GUIDANCE:
Dear God, please help me to overcome any evil in
my life with your help. Thank you for constantly
protecting me and for giving me righteousness.

More Than a Conqueror

*"No, in all these things we are more than
conquerors through him who loved us."*
Romans 8:37 NIV

Do you remember that you are more than a conqueror through Jesus? Sometimes in your life, you will feel less than adequate and less than worthy in God's eyes. But He wants you to know that He sees you as more than a conqueror throughout your life. You can do great and amazing things, and you have been able to do them ever since you came to know God. You were able to get through seemingly impossible times, and you were able to conquer hard times at work, within your family, and in your personal life.

Whatever Satan puts in your head is not true. You are not a lost cause. You are not too far gone to ever receive forgiveness. You are not too far gone to know that things can and will turn around for you. You are not a mistake, and you never were a mistake. God doesn't make mistakes. He knows that you can and will rise again after any challenge knocks you down. Let each challenge make you wiser, stronger, and more aware of what is happening around you. Let each obstacle help you become a better person. You are loved in more ways than you will ever know by God, your friends, and your family.

There is nothing that God won't deliver you from. He wants to give you the strength to withstand life's challenges in His ways. His way is the best way to get through any obstacle that is in front of you. You can walk through, around, or in the middle of any hard time, you face and know deep in your heart that you can and will get through it. Tell yourself, "I can get through this. I can and will become wiser and stronger. God is with me. I am more than a conqueror through Jesus."

Prayer for Help:
Dear God, please help me have the mindset that I
am more than a conqueror through you. Thank you
that I can conquer anything in your name.

HE WILL BE WITH YOU

*"But if God so clothes the grass of the field, which today
is alive and tomorrow is thrown into the oven, will he
not much more clothe you, O you of little faith?"*
Mathew 6:30 ESV

You have no doubt gone through difficult times in your life. However, God has sustained you in every possible way. He has brought you through tough times with peace in your heart as you learned to trust in Him. Your hope overflows that the best part of your life is yet to come. You have the hope of eternal life flowing inside you at all times. All you have to do is call on Him to remind you of His promises, and He will hear you.

Whenever you are close to giving up hope, remember this scripture and the promise that He makes to you. If God cares about the grass of the fields, which is here today and gone tomorrow, He also hears you whenever you call on Him, whether it's day or night. He wants to give you the hope that can't be extinguished. Even though your faith will be tested in ways you never expected, God wants you to keep the faith and the hope alive in your heart. You will have little faith at certain times, but God will restore your faith and hope. God even asks you in the scripture, "if I can take care of the grass of the fields, don't you think I can and will take care of you and clothe you? O you of little faith?" This means that you will doubt God and His plan for your life, but He still is there with you in the midst of hard times. He wants to reassure you that you will be taken care of by Him all the days of your life, from the time you were born up until now. God can take care of you in ways that you never expected.

PRAYER OF GUIDANCE:
Dear God, please help me to keep my faith and
hope strong. Thank you for always putting hope
back into my heart whenever I need a boost.

NOTHING WILL HARM YOU

"I have given you authority to trample on snakes and scorpions and to overcome all the power of the enemy; nothing will harm you."
Luke 10:19 NIV

You have great power within you. You have the power to trample on any snakes and scorpions that come onto your path of life. In Biblical times this meant that God was giving people the ability to trample on snakes and scorpions in their paths because they were walking on dangerous roads while spreading the Gospel to many different lands. It also meant that God gave people the ability to get through any obstacles that came their way.

This verse still holds just as much truth today as it did more than 2,000 years ago. It gives you the ability and authority to defeat any enemy that crosses your path. Cling to the hope that God has given you by His mercy every day, instead of giving in to the sting of people's words and actions, or lack thereof. God tells you in the scripture that as long as you cling to Him, nothing will harm you. You can trample on any negative thoughts that enter your mind and counteract them with good thoughts about your future. You have the power to overcome anything the enemy has put in your path. He is an enemy that will try to sting you with lies, negative thoughts, and self-doubt. As long as you trust in God, nothing will ever be too difficult for you to overcome. You will trample upon anyone that tries to feed you lies about your life because you will know deep in your heart that you are God's child. Nothing can ever separate you from His love. You will withstand the power of any and every enemy because you have the power of God residing in you.

PRAYER OF GRATITUDE:
Dear God, thank you for giving me power over all enemies through my faith. Help me to remember that through you, I'm able to conquer anything that crosses my path.

The Good Fight of Faith

"Fight the good fight of the faith. Take hold of the eternal life to which you were called when you made your good confession in the presence of many witnesses."
1Timothy 6:12 NIV

Fighting the good fight of faith is something that you have to work on every day of your life. Keeping the faith is a battle. You have to remind yourself to keep the faith even when it seems as if things are spiraling out of control. Fighting for your faith means standing strong when everyone else in the world calls you crazy for believing in the One true God. Fighting the good fight of faith means being an encouragement to people who are struggling and helping them understand that their struggles are only temporary. They are nothing compared to the beauty that is coming after the storms in their life pass. Whenever someone is going through a hard time, you can encourage them by telling them the pain won't last forever. Remind them of all the other times that God has come through for them and remind them of the promise they have through their faith in God. You can even remind yourself that you are always fighting the good fight even when hard times come upon you.

Cling to the eternal life that you have in Jesus Christ. Think back to the day you accepted Jesus Christ as your Lord and Savior. Think back to how happy and at peace you were in that moment. You confessed with your mouth and heart that Jesus Christ is the Lord of your life. Everyone around you started rejoicing. Whenever hard times come, remember that God will help you fight to stay strong. Fight the good fight and cling to God for the strength and the hope you need. He will give you the ability to fight the good fight every day. Embrace your ability to fight the good fight of faith.

Prayer of Relief:
Dear God, thank you that I was able to confess that you are my Savior in front of my friends and family. Please help me to cling to my faith. Help me to always want to fight the good fight of faith.

ARMED WITH STRENGTH

*"You armed me with strength for battle;
you humbled my adversaries before me."*
Psalm 18:39 NIV

No matter how hard things seem, you are armed with strength from God. That means that you can and will get through challenges with God at your side no matter what you face. There will be hard battles that you face in your life, but you can cling to the hope that God gives you. He loves you and places the ability to fight any battle within you as soon as you accepted Him as your Savior. God humbles people that were thinking of harming you in any way. He lets you go through trials that test you and strengthen your reliance on Him. Come before Him and ask Him for the strength you need to face each day's challenges head-on. He will get you through anything that comes your way. He humbles your adversaries before you every day. Maybe your boss was getting ready to yell at you, and He intervened. Maybe you were getting ready to yell at your spouse or your kids, and He told you to take a breather. Maybe a friend was able to start gossiping about you, and He got them to stop. Whenever you are struggling, God will help you by carrying you through when you feel you can't take another step.

He will strengthen you every day of your life in ways that you can't even fathom. When you get to the other side of your struggles and can smile again, that is when you will look up at God and say, "Lord, thank you for carrying me through another trial. It is by your grace that I made it through to the other side." Being armed with strength means knowing that you are stronger than you seem. You can do more than you ever thought possible with God at your side.

PRAYER OF COMFORT:
Dear God, thank you for arming me with strength
for any battle that I face. Whenever challenges arise,
please help me remember that you humbled my
enemies before me and that you will do it again.

WHAT CAN MAN DO?

"The Lord is on my side; I will not fear. What can man do to me?"
Psalm 118:6 ESV

It can be hard to remember that God is on your side during rough times. It can seem as though He is distant, not listening, and even ignoring you altogether. But the exact opposite is true. He is right there with you in the middle of your darkest days and in your most difficult time. He sees your pain, hears your tears and cries, and moves mountains when you feel as though you will be stuck between a rock and a hard place forever. You might deal with fear and anxiety during your most difficult time. But instead of giving in to despair, you can have the peace and confidence that God is with you.

The Lord is truly on your side at all times because right when you think you're in a situation where it's the end-all, be-all, that's when God will help you and uplift you in the most unexpected ways. Whether it's a kind smile from a stranger, a family member, or a friend calling you out of nowhere to see how you're doing, or one of your neighbors bringing you dinner out of the goodness of their hearts, God will help you see that you're not alone. He never sends you into a situation without His help. He will help you know that He is with you by giving you the strength to face every day with optimism. He helps you be kind to unkind people, and He helps you enjoy your life even though it can be difficult. Going through the difficulties with a smile on your face will help you know that none of the hard times last forever. Even though you will feel discouraged, you can remind yourself that this world could do nothing that God won't work through to help you understand His love for you.

PRAYER OF RELIEF:
Dear Lord, please help me remember that there is nothing
man can do to me when I'm centered on your hope and love.

He Delivers You

"Though I walk in the midst of trouble, you preserve my life;
you stretch out your hand against the wrath of my enemies,
and your right hand delivers me."
Psalm 138:7 ESV

Even though this life can and will cause you trouble, God is the one who sustains you. When you think that you're down to your last ounce of strength, that's when He says to you, "my child try again. Walk with me through any struggles that you have." He has saved your life more than once, from the second you accepted Him as your Lord and Savior. He has helped you walk through trials that other people would have easily given up during. He gives you the inner strength to persevere and to never give up. Whenever you feel as though you are surrounded by your enemies on all sides, that is when God stretches out His hand to deliver you from them. You can then walk through your life with your enemies looking at you, wondering why and how you are still standing. You know deep in your heart that Jesus has delivered you from many hard times before, and He will do it again. He will deliver you with His right hand, and He will fill you with the hope that can't be explained in the human sense.

His hope will calm your senses, help you think clearly, and it will help you make good decisions about the next step you are supposed to take in life. It will help you realize that His plan is much better than your plan. His hope can help you do things that you never thought possible, like a walk through the difficult times with a smile on your face. God has saved you from your enemies by giving you a way out when there seemed to be no way out. The next time you face an enemy, automatically go to God and ask Him to help you through that situation. Then wait and see how He shows up for you.

PRAYER OF GRATITUDE:
Dear Lord, thank you for delivering me from my enemies. Thank you for helping me through rough times. Help me to focus on you.

Being Aware of Satan

"Be sober-minded; be watchful. Your adversary the devil prowls around like a roaring lion, seeking someone to devour. Resist him, firm in your faith, knowing that the same kinds of suffering are being ßexperienced by your brotherhood throughout the world."
1 Peter 5:8-9 ESV

Be aware of your surroundings at all times. Your enemy, the devil, prowls around like a hungry lion every day, looking for someone to devour. You can resist him in many ways by holding on to your faith. Hold on to Jesus with every last bit of strength you have. Everyone in the world has been tempted, tested, and tried in the same ways you have. They have had their faith shaken to the very core of its foundation. They have felt like giving up and saying that they couldn't do it anymore. The devil attacks everyone every day. That is why it's so important to stand firm in your faith in Jesus and remind yourself that there is a way out of the devil's traps through Him. God can and will help you resist the devil by helping you remember to turn to Him whenever times seem to be too difficult to handle. Your temptations are the same as everyone else's, but the difference is that you have the hope of God and the peace of God at your fingertips.

Whenever you call on God, He hears you and helps you resist the devil. He helps you resist the devil by turning your eyes and your mind towards Him. Whenever Satan tempts you to look at the stressors of your life, God reminds you to look at the blessings in life. Whenever Satan tries to make you dread a situation at work, God reminds you what a privilege it is to be working in your field. Whenever you think you are the only one getting tested every day, God reminds you that everyone gets tempted, but it's up to you to keep your hope in Him as the One who will get you through trials.

Prayer for Guidance:
Dear God, please help me remember to focus on
you the next time the devil tempts me. Help me
to resist him and remember your promises.

Work for The Lord

"But thanks be to God, who gives us the victory through our
Lord Jesus Christ. Therefore, my beloved brothers, be steadfast,
immovable, always abounding in the work of the Lord,
knowing that in the Lord your labor is not in vain."
1 Corinthians 15:57-58 ESV

At times it can feel like you're laboring in vain throughout your life. You're left wondering if all of your hard work is worth it. You ask yourself, "can I make a difference and point others to Christ? How can I keep going like this if I haven't seen any real progress? Who will listen to me about the amazing things God has done?" But God has ways of making all of your hard work worth it. He helps you focus on the victory that you have through your Lord and Savior, Jesus Christ. God wants you to know that even though your life feels exhausting, your hard work is not in vain.

As long as you do everything for His glory and you stay focused on Him, that will help you persevere through hard times. You can be steadfast in your faith and be immovable when Satan tries to attack you through your hard times. Instead of giving in to him, you can say things such as, "God's love for me outweighs your lies." "You aren't going to take my faith away from me. I know God loves me and died for me on the cross." "I know God is for me, so no harm will come to me. He gave me the victory through faith in Jesus."

Whenever you work for the Lord, you know that you will face trials of many sorts. But you can cling to the hope that God sees you working with all your heart to bring other people to know Him and have a relationship with Him. You know that people will see God through your words and actions. Some will ask Him into their hearts because of you. None of your work is in vain.

Prayer for Worried:
Dear God, please help me know that my hard work
of leading others to you is never in vain.

Look Forward with Hope

"Why are you cast down, O my soul, and why are you in turmoil within me? Hope in God; for I shall again praise him, my salvation."
Psalm 42:5 ESV

Have you ever asked yourself why you were so sad, disheartened, discouraged, stressed out, and uncertain about how things in your life were going? What conclusions did you come up with? Maybe you're uncertain because of financial issues or discouraged because of the pressures of work. Maybe you're feeling doubts about your abilities and the way God made you. Or, maybe you're dealing with some tough family issues that you are just not sure how you will get through. The good news is that whenever you're in turmoil mentally and emotionally, God is right there in the middle of it all with you.

He asks you why you are so downcast in your spirit because He wants to see you happy again and having that spring in your step that you used to have. He wants you to remember to come to Him for the hope that you need in your heart. He wants you to return to Him and have a relationship with Him. A relationship with Him is the most important relationship that you can have. Hoping in Jesus means trusting in His plan even if you don't understand it. So, even if you don't understand why things aren't working out the way you would like, that is the perfect time to turn back to the hope that you had in God before things start to unravel. That's the time to turn to God and say, "Lord, I know I can't do this life on my own. Please help me." Knowing God is the key to your everlasting sense of certainty. You will know for certain that you are safe in God's arms and that you can cling to Him no matter what. You don't have to be downcast but instead, look forward to everything in your life with hope in your heart.

Prayer of Relief:
Dear God, please help me turn to you whenever I
feel like my life is in turmoil. Thank you for being
my ultimate source of certainty and hope.